CHRISTIAN BE

Christian Beliefs

AN INTRODUCTORY STUDY GUIDE

I. HOWARD MARSHALL

INTER-VARSITY PRESS

Inter-Varsity Press
Inter-Varsity Fellowship,
39 Bedford Square, London WC1B 3EY

First Edition September 1963
Reprinted May 1964
Reprinted March 1966
Second Edition March 1969
Reprinted June 1972

International Standard Book Number
0 85110 320 0

Printed in Great Britain by
Hazell Watson & Viney Ltd, Aylesbury, Bucks

CONTENTS

PREFACE

When beginning the study of a new subject it is useful to obtain a bird's-eye view of the whole before concentrating on any one section in greater detail. The study of Christian doctrine is no exception. This small book seeks to provide the kind of simple, brief, straightforward introduction to the subject which many Christians find that they need.

An attempt has been made to cover all the main doctrines of the Christian faith, although inevitably many important matters have been treated with the utmost brevity. As far as possible technical terms have been explained, and philosophical questions have been left strictly alone. Although there may be found places which, like certain parts of Paul's Epistles, are 'hard to understand', it is hoped that these will yield to study, and that the impression has not been given that theology is an obscure and recondite subject suitable only for dry-as-dust professors locked up in theological seminaries!

It should perhaps be stressed that this is a work-book. It is not intended that it should be read from start to finish at one sitting. The method employed has been to expound scriptural teaching systematically; fairly full references, especially from the New Testament, have been given, and since they are an essential part of the study and are meant to be turned up when the book is being studied, they have been placed deliberately within the text itself and not relegated to footnotes.

Reference has also been made to a longer passage at the head of nearly every section. This has been done for two reasons: first, this should help to obviate the well-known danger of studying doctrine on the basis of proof-texts isolated from their contexts; second, such references will provide suitable passages for group or individual Bible study on each aspect of Christian doctrine. In this connection, also, questions for discussion have been provided at the end of each chapter. Biblical quotations are normally taken from the Revised Standard Version.

This book will have served its purpose if it whets the appetite for more detailed study of its subject. T. C. Hammond's handbook on Christian doctrine, 'In Understanding Be Men', will be found extremely useful for this purpose, and individual doctrines can also be studied with the help of some of the books and booklets in the bibliography on p. 91.

In the early stages of preparation much valuable help was given by the Rev. Donald English, and the author would like to express his grateful thanks to him and to all others who have helped in the compiling of this book.

I. Howard Marshall

Introduction

THE STUDY OF CHRISTIAN DOCTRINE

The purpose of this book is to set out briefly and systematically the doctrines which comprise the Christian faith and which are believed by Christians.

It is not immediately obvious that this is a subject in which every Christian ought to be interested. Many people may well think that the **study** of Christian doctrine ought to be left to ministers and lecturers who have a professional interest in that kind of thing. Is it not enough, it may be asked, simply to be a Christian and believe in Jesus Christ without getting lost in the mysteries of theology?

Reasons for studying Christian doctrine (Read Ephesians 1:15-23)

Can we really ignore Christian doctrine? We do so at our peril, for it is only by a study of it that we can hope to grow in the Christian life.

Christian doctrine is basically quite simple; it is an attempt to set out systematically all that we know about God through His Word. And clearly it is vital for us to know as much as possible about the character of God and His plan for our lives if we are to enjoy to the full His purpose for us.

There are some people who never experience the full blessings of belief in Jesus Christ simply because they do not know that they exist. A man may get a considerable amount of fun out of tinkering with radio sets, but he will never get the best out of his hobby until he has read and studied the theory of radio. In the same way we cannot get the best out of Christianity unless we know something of the 'theory' underlying it.

A study of doctrine is also necessary to prevent us from falling into errors which may seriously affect our conduct. There are many examples of Christians who have been led astray into the most queer behaviour simply because they were not sufficiently well-instructed to be able to distinguish between true and false doctrine. In the sixteenth century, for example, some Christians practised polygamy out of a mistaken understanding of the gospel. Some people today misunderstand the relationship between the Jewish Sabbath and the Christian Lord's Day, and this leads them to observe Saturday as their day of rest instead of Sunday. The antidote to such peculiarities of behaviour is a sound knowledge of Christian doctrine.

Again, all Christians are called by God to be witnesses to Jesus Christ and to spread the gospel in the world. But this cannot be done by people who do not understand the gospel themselves. A person who does not understand the basic principles of, say, pacifism will hardly be able to convince other people that they ought to be pacifists; similarly nobody can be a successful evangelist without knowing and understanding the 'evangel', the gospel.

Hence we may say that Christian doctrine is the concern of every Christian who is determined to grow in the Christian life, to avoid error, and to propagate his faith. Naturally not every Christian can aspire to being a great theologian, but every Christian has the duty to have as deep a knowledge of theology as he is capable of.

We ought to remember, however, that a thorough knowledge of doctrine will not of itself make us good Christians. The man who knows all the theory of radio may not be the most expert of workmen when it comes to the practical business of mending my set for me. And it is sadly possible for what we learn with our heads never to affect our hearts and lives, or for us to be filled only with pride in our knowledge. We must always be humble in our study and take care to apply what we learn to our everyday lives.

What is Christian doctrine? (Acts 18 : 24-28)

We have come this far without having stated what Christian doctrine is, although various hints about it have been dropped. Our main clue is that the word 'doctrine' literally means 'teaching', so that Christian doctrine is what Christians teach. We can look at this from three points of view.

First, Christian doctrine is **a statement of the things which Christians believe.** When a person says, 'I believe that . . .', he is expressing what he believes, *i.e.* Christian doctrine. We can find summaries of such belief in the various creeds and confessions of the church: for example, the Apostles', Nicene, and Athanasian Creeds and the Thirty-Nine Articles which will be found set out in the Anglican Prayer Book, and the Westminster Confession of the Presbyterian Churches. In the same way movements such as the Inter-Varsity Fellowship have a doctrinal basis written into their constitution. Doctrine, then, is a systematic and orderly statement of what Christians believe about God and the world.

But we know that a man does not become a Christian simply by believing certain things in his head about God. To his head-knowledge must be added heart-knowledge. He must have a personal trust in God through Jesus Christ. This raises the question: what does it mean to have a personal trust in God? To give an answer to that question is, of course, to state Christian doctrine. Thus, second, doctrine is **a statement of what it means to have personal trust in God.**

How do we know about God and what it means to trust in Him? The answer is that we know this through what God has revealed to us about Himself and His purposes for mankind. He has spoken to us in His Word, which for all practical purposes means, as we shall see, the Bible. Consequently, our third definition of doctrine is in terms of its source, and states that Christian doctrine is **an exposition of God's revelation of Himself in the Bible.** But this theme is sufficiently important to require a section to itself.

The Bible and Christian doctrine (Acts 17:1–12)

At this point somebody may come forward with an important question. If we already have God's revelation in the Bible, it may be asked, why do we need to study doctrine? Is it not enough to be a Bible student without bothering about doctrine? Perhaps the answer to this question is that anybody who studies the Bible is in fact really studying doctrine! But something more than that needs to be said.

The Bible is a record of God's revelation arranged historically rather than systematically. This means, for example, that the teaching of the Bible about, say, creation is not confined (as is often thought) to the first chapters of Genesis; many important things are said about creation in such places as Psalm 8, Isaiah 40 and Colossians 1. In order to understand the doctrine of creation, therefore, it is necessary to assemble all the passages in the Bible which deal with it, to compare them with each other and to arrive at a comprehensive statement of what the Bible says on that theme.

We can hardly begin to study the Bible without resorting to systematic work of this kind, or, in other words, to 'systematic theology'. Even this, of course, is not all that there is to theology. We must also take into account what has been said by philosophers and scientists on such a topic as creation and relate the teaching of the Bible to their discoveries. But in this book we shall confine ourselves mainly to the teaching of the Bible.

Christian doctrine is thus a method by which we understand the message of the Bible, and no Christian can possibly neglect it. This raises the question: how are we to use the Bible in our study of doctrine? What is the **method** used by the theologian?

The **first** point is that the Bible is to be the chief source used by the student of doctrine. It is there (as we shall see) that God has revealed Himself to us most fully, since the Bible is the record of how God spoke to men in His Son, Jesus Christ. Although, therefore, we may learn something about God from the world around us, from the history of mankind and from the writings of great men, our ultimate and supreme source, by which all other sources must be tested, is the Bible (see 2 Jn. 9).

A **second** point is that we need to study the message of the Bible as a whole and not take texts out of their context. We all know stories of people who have taken texts at random and read their own meaning into them with comical or even tragic results. It is always safest to study whole passages rather than isolated texts, and to 'compare scripture with scripture'.

Third, it is not enough to study the Bible alone. It would be sheer folly to ignore the collective wisdom of the church down the ages, the labours of commentators and theologians who have expounded the meaning of the Bible, according to their varying ability. Naturally this does not mean that we follow them blindly; even the best of commentators can make mistakes. But by careful use of their works we can attain to a far deeper knowledge of the truth than we could simply by our own efforts.

Human knowledge and insight are, however, not enough. We ought, **fourth,** to pray for the illumination of the Spirit of God so that we may have the aid of the Author in understanding His Book. There can be no better commentator than He.

Finally, it should not be forgotten that much of Christian doctrine is too deep for us to understand. For how can men fully understand the mind of their God and Creator? We should not be surprised if we find mysteries which we cannot fathom, and this should also serve as a warning to us not to be content with easy and superficial answers to difficult questions.

A word about the **plan of the book** should perhaps be added. Christian doctrine centres round two great themes: first, the character of God and of the world which He has created, and, second, the new creation, in which He undoes the effects of sin on the first creation. This determines the structure of the following sections:

After looking in greater detail at the way in which we learn about God (section 1), we shall consider what in fact we do know about God (section 2) and about the world which He has created and the sin which has invaded it (section 3).

Then we discuss His new creation—its beginning, which centres in Jesus Christ, who He is and what He has done for us (section 4); its outworking in the individual Christian (section 5) and in the church (section 6); and its final completion at the second advent of Jesus Christ (section 7).

QUESTIONS FOR DISCUSSION

1. A Unitarian minister once put up a poster saying that he offered 'religion without dogma'. Do you think that what he offered is possible?

2. Would you agree that a person cannot be an effective preacher without being a student of Christian doctrine?

3. What do you understand by 'doctrinal preaching'? Do you think that it is sufficiently practised in the church today?

4. Is it possible for a person who is not himself a Christian to understand Christian doctrine fully? Give reasons for your answer.

5. It has been said that 'deep theology is the best fuel for devotion'; discuss.

Section 1

OUR KNOWLEDGE OF GOD

Christian doctrine tells us what Christians believe about God. But before we can discuss what we believe about God we must ask how we come to know about Him and to learn about His existence, character and actions.

The simplest answer to this question is that we know about God only because He has revealed Himself to us.

Left to himself, man could not learn about God because he is a creature of limited ability and understanding, and unable to comprehend the greatness of God; he is also a sinful and imperfect being, who is prevented by his sin from understanding a holy and righteous God.

But in His kindness God has revealed Himself to finite and sinful men. He has shown something of His character **in the universe which He has made,** and **in the way in which He controls human history.** Yet these two ways of revelation are too general to tell men very much about the character of God, and too impersonal to bring them into living fellowship with Him. God has, therefore, used two other avenues of revelation to speak to men—**the life and work of His Son Jesus Christ,** and **the Holy Scriptures.** This means that we have four ways of divine revelation to consider in this section. Then we must also say something about the way in which men respond to God's revelation.

GOD'S REVELATION OF HIMSELF TO MEN

Revelation in nature (Isaiah 40)

In almost every age men have been led to believe in and to worship some power or powers greater than themselves as a result of considering the nature of the world around them (see Ps. 19:1).

The reasons for believing in God in this way have been called 'proofs' by philosophers and many attempts have been made down the years to state them clearly and convincingly. It has been argued, for example, that the very fact that the universe exists implies that it must have a creator; or that the presence of beauty and design in the universe proves that there was a designer who created it; or that the existence of such ideas as goodness, justice and love in a material universe suggests the existence of a moral and spiritual Being who created them.

Scholars, however, still debate whether these 'proofs' really prove the existence of God. At the very least they show that the universe is hardly self-explanatory or self-sufficient. They show that belief in God is not unreasonable or silly, and they confirm a belief in God based on other grounds. The facts remain, however, that not everybody is convinced by these proofs and that they tell us very little about the character of God. We may regard them as ways in which men hear the voice of God speaking to them through the universe which He created, but in order to hear His voice more clearly we must turn to other forms of revelation.

Revelation in history (Psalm 78)

The second way in which God has revealed Himself to men is through history, and in particular through the history of the nation of Israel. This people claimed that God (whom they called 'Yahweh'—our 'Jehovah') was active in their individual and national life.

He used the prophets as His spokesmen (1 Sa. 3; Is. 6; Ho. 1; Am. 7:14 f.), and revealed that His character was righteous and loving (Is. 6:3; Am. 5:6 f.; Dt. 7:8; Je. 31:3; Ho. 11:1), that the nation of Israel was His chosen people (Dt. 7:7 f.; Je. 7:23; 13:11), and that He required of them not only worship but also righteousness and love in their social and national life (Am. 5:21–24; Is. 1:27; Mi. 6:8).

This God was Lord over creation (Is. 40; 42:5; Am. 5:8) and the moral ruler of history (Dt. 28; Jdg. 2; Am. 5:14). One day He would judge the world and set up a kingdom of righteousness. His ultimate purpose for men was thus salvation, and to this end He had chosen Israel to be His servant in bringing true religion to all men. But because Israel was spoilt for this task by sin He promised to raise up a future deliverer, described variously as a king in the succession of

David or as the servant of the Lord (Is. 2:1–4; 9:1–7; 11:1–9; 42:1–9; 49:1–6; 50:4–9; 52:13–53:12; Je. 31:31 ff.; 33:14–16; Ezk. 34; 37).

This revelation is more explicit and more informative about the personal character of God than is the revelation through nature. Yet it, too, is in itself incomplete and can be fully understood only in the light of the third method of revelation employed by God, the life and work of Jesus Christ.

Revelation in Jesus Christ (John 5:19–47)

The coming of Jesus Christ was the supreme manifestation and fulfilment of the revelation which God had begun to make in the life of Israel. He claimed explicitly to be the One whom the prophets foretold (Mt. 5:17; Lk. 24:44). He spoke of Himself as the Son of God (Mt. 11:25–27), and He ascribed the authority of God Himself to His words (Mk. 2:1–12; 13:31; 14:62).

But it was not only in His words that Jesus claimed to reveal God. His character and actions were also intended to be regarded as a manifestation of God to men. His miracles and mighty works were signs of this manifestation (Lk. 12:54–56; Jn. 3:2; 14:11). His whole life displayed the love which was characteristic of His Father (Mk. 2:17; 10:21,45; Lk. 19:1–10), His death crowned His life of self-giving for men (Mk. 14:22–24), and His resurrection and ascension declared that God was pleased with the work of His Son and had exalted Him (Acts 3:14 f.; Rom. 1:4). His disciples spent the rest of their lives preaching Him as the One who truly revealed God to men and restored them to a right relationship with Him. The impressive evidence of His influence upon human lives ever since further bears out His claim to reveal God to men.

Such a revelation in which God became a man in His Son Jesus Christ is a personal revelation. It is unrepeatable and perfect. Jesus is in the fullest sense the Word of God (Jn. 1:1–18).

Revelation in the Bible (Revelation 1)

If Jesus is the supreme revelation of God, the problem now

arises: how can God reveal Himself to us who live so long after the time of Jesus? Are we unable to receive the full revelation of God?

There is, however, a further form of revelation in which the Spirit of God enables men to bear witness in writing to the revelation which they have received so that they can interpret it and pass it on to later generations. We are thus able to come to a knowledge of God's revelation in nature, in history and in Jesus Christ through the record of it which we have in the Bible. This record is itself to be regarded as a revelation of God through which He speaks to men today.

In this way Jesus Christ still reveals Himself to men. He is not a dead man of the past but the living Son of God, and Christians who live in the time after His crucifixion are able to say that they know Him and have fellowship with Him.

Since, therefore, the Bible is the means normally used by God to reveal Himself to men today, we must consider with some care its character, reliability and sufficiency as a revelation of God.

THE BIBLE AS DIVINE REVELATION

The Old Testament (Jeremiah 36)

The Old Testament is the record of the first great episode of revelation, God's dealings with Israel. It outlines the history of Israel in such a way as to bring out its significant features, and it preserves the sayings and writings of men to whom God revealed Himself.

The various books which make up this library of thirty-nine volumes were compiled and collected over a period of centuries. By the time of Jesus the Jews had come to accept and set apart these books as the authoritative revelation of God. The process of 'canonization' of the Old Testament (i.e., of accepting these books and only these books as the 'canon', or authoritative list, of Scripture) by the Jews is generally reckoned to have been completed by the Council of Jamnia just before AD 100, but this council was really endorsing opinions arrived at much earlier.

The New Testament (John 16:12–15)

The Christian church followed the example of Jesus in taking over the Jewish sacred Scriptures as its own authoritative documents (Lk. 24:27,44). It also set aside its own distinctive sacred books out of a large mass of available material. The New Testament was thus formed, consisting of twenty-seven books, written by the apostles and their associates, which recorded the life of Jesus and the story of the early church.

The books which made up the New Testament were books which were recognized by the church as carrying the stamp of divine authority. Consequently the process of canonization was not so much a conferring of authority by the church upon these books as a recognition of the authority which they inherently possessed. As in the case of the Old Testament, the process of canonization took some time; it was virtually complete by AD 367, but long before this date the great bulk of the New Testament had been accepted by the church as Scripture.

The inspiration of the Bible (2 Timothy 3:14–17)

There are two reasons why the Bible is able to reveal God to men. The first is that it is a record of His acts of revelation in the history of Israel and in the ministry of Jesus Christ (Jn. 20:30 f.). The second is that God is its ultimate author, so that He is able to speak through the Bible to men. We may say that the Bible is the Word of God expressed in a written form.

The Bible is, of course, a human book, written by men. But at the same time it is the work of men to whom the Word of God was revealed. Naturally this happened in different ways. Sometimes the writers simply recorded historical events; sometimes they recorded the messages which prophets and apostles received from God; sometimes they pondered deeply in their own minds on the things of God and He used their thoughts to bring His message to men; and sometimes they were guided by God to write words that were charged with a deeper meaning than they themselves were aware of (1 Pet. 1:10–12; cf. Dn. 12:8 f.). While the

Bible is the work of human authors, it is nevertheless divine in origin and can be described as 'God-breathed' (see 2 Tim. 3: 16); its authors are men who were moved by the Holy Spirit (2 Pet. 1 : 20 f.; cf. Rev. 19 : 9; 22 : 6).

Acceptance of the Bible as the Word of God is not a matter of rigid scientific proof but of faith. This does not mean that we adopt an attitude which is irrational and without foundation. Rather, our attitude is based on acceptance of the testimony of Jesus to the Old Testament and on the Bible's own witness regarding its nature. Such an attitude is confirmed by our own experience that we hear the Word of God in the Bible. We may perhaps compare the way in which our acceptance of Jesus Christ as the Son of God does not rest ultimately upon man-made proofs of His divinity but is an act of faith. Such an act of faith, however, does not relieve us of the responsibility of examining the arguments which may be brought against our faith. We must look in more detail at some of these arguments.

First, it is often said that written statements or words may be used to tell us about acts of revelation but cannot themselves be a revelation, since revelation is held to occur only through events and in persons; consequently, the Bible may be a book about revelation but not itself a revelation of God.

But this argument ignores the fact that one of the chief ways in which persons reveal themselves to each other is by conversation—i.e. by words. God, who is a Person, was not content to use events to reveal Himself to us but employed words which He gave to His prophets (e.g. Dt. 4: 1–5; 2 Sa. 23 : 2; Je. 1 : 9). When He revealed Himself in the Person of Jesus, He again made much use of words: the Gospel writers are as much interested in what Jesus said as in what He did, and, according to John, He claimed that His words were the words (or word) of God (Jn. 7 : 16 f.; 8 : 38; 14 : 24; 17 : 8,14). Again, the characteristic way in which the early church brought men face to face with Jesus was by preaching. Words are undoubtedly one of the ways in which God reveals Himself to men (cf. 1 Cor. 2 : 13).

Second, it may be objected that on the view which has been outlined the human writers of the Bible were simply passive instruments, like typewriters, used by God to record what

He wished. But it is no more true to say this than to say that Jesus behaved like a divine tape-recorder when He spoke. The truth is that the word of God came to the biblical writers in many different ways, but usually through the normal exercise of their God-given faculties of mind and reason. There is undoubtedly a paradox here in that we can regard the Bible as at once a human book and a divine book. But it is the same kind of paradox as the belief that Jesus was an ordinary man and at the same time the Son of God. Indeed we may legitimately use this analogy to help us to understand the nature of the Bible, provided that we do not fall into bibliolatry, the error of regarding the Bible as a kind of incarnation of the Holy Spirit and so worshipping it.

Third, it is asked whether it is right to say that the whole of the Bible is inspired or that God speaks equally through all parts of it. Here it is important to remember that the church accepted and set apart a canon of Scripture. By doing so it expressly denied the inspiration of many other books which dealt with the history of Israel and the early church, and it equally expressly affirmed that the books which were accepted were inspired by God. Christian experience has found that God does reveal Himself to men throughout the Bible, although He does so much more clearly in some parts (e.g. John) than in others (e.g. Ecclesiastes) which are, we may say, peripheral to His supreme revelation in Jesus Christ. Again, even if some parts of the Bible do not seem to have a message for us in our situation, it is quite possible that they may have spoken or will speak to other people in other situations. We may compare the way in which the book of Revelation has come to life again and again for Christians enduring persecution. Finally, the Bible itself does not encourage us to divide it up into parts, but to regard it as an organic whole, each book having a part to play in the whole work.

The reliability and infallibility of the Bible (Luke 1:1–4)

Christians have traditionally held that the Bible, as a book inspired by God, is a fully reliable revelation of God. This claim is based on the attitude of Jesus to the Old Testament and on the witness of the Bible to its own character (Mt. 5:17,18; Mk. 7:1–13; 12:35–37; Jn. 5:39–47; 10:34–36; 1 Cor. 14:37 f.; Eph. 3:3), and is a corollary of the belief that the Bible is inspired by God. Like belief in inspiration, therefore, belief in the reliability of the Bible is a matter of faith and not of proof, but at the same time such belief can be defended by the ordinary methods of historical study.

It is true that we are often told that this belief is no longer tenable by modern Christians, and that we cannot believe in the reliability of the Bible because of the many alleged errors and contradictions which it contains. We must therefore state the following points by way of elucidation of this belief.

First, the Bible is held to be a full and reliable revelation only of God. It is not meant to be an infallible encyclopaedia of information on all subjects, and therefore it does not provide answers to all the questions which we ask about the world around us. Its purpose is primarily to train and instruct men in the Christian faith.

Second, the Bible is written in popular language and not with twentieth-century scientific terminology and exactitude. Indeed it would be foolish to expect the latter; and if, by some miracle, it had been achieved, it would then be unintelligible to most of us, and to all who had come before us, and would very soon be hopelessly out of date.

Third, it records a developing revelation of God over many centuries to many different people. We must not, therefore, take its statements in isolation from each other but consider them in the light of the whole. We cannot base our beliefs on individual sentences taken out of their context.

Fourth, it is a fact that, by and large, modern archaeological science has done a great deal to confirm the accuracy of the history recorded in the Bible, and only rarely and in relatively unimportant matters does it put a question mark against the biblical record. Since the Bible records a revelation which took place through history, we can be glad that the historical outline presented in the Bible is capable of so much archaeological verification.

Fifth, many of the alleged difficulties in the Bible are due to our failure to interpret it correctly. We may, for example, look for literal statements in passages which are meant to be taken as poetic. Through a full understanding of the Bible we may find that many discrepancies vanish or are trivial in regard to the truth of the Bible seen as a whole.

When these factors are taken into account, it will be seen that belief in the reliability, or, to use the traditional term, the infallibility, of the Bible is not as ill-founded as many people today think it to be. There are, of course, difficulties surrounding the belief, just as there are many difficulties surrounding belief in the love of God in a universe where evil and pain are so common, but we may well doubt whether these difficulties are sufficient to overthrow a doctrine which is testified to in the Bible itself.

The interpretation of the Bible (2 Peter 3:15–18)

Belief that the Bible is a fully reliable revelation of God does not necessarily guarantee a true apprehension of that revelation by its readers. We need to remember, for example, that not all of the Bible is meant to be taken literally. Some parts are written in poetic or symbolic language (e.g. the Psalms and Revelation) and some of its narratives are to be regarded as fiction (e.g. several of the parables). It is necessary to exercise much care and caution in the interpretation of the Bible and to avoid the assumption that our own interpretation of any particular passage is the only correct one. We are to use all the mental resources we possess and the insights of devout scholars as we seek to understand the Bible. (On this subject see Alan M. Stibbs, 'Understanding God's Word', Inter-Varsity Press.)

There is consequently a fully legitimate place for biblical criticism, by which we mean the reverent study of the various books of the Bible in order to determine their background, structure, date, authorship, and relation to other writings. Caution is necessary, however, since it is easy to approach such study with unwarranted presuppositions which may lead to false conclusions regarding the composition and truth of the Bible. Scrupulous Christian honesty is required in biblical criticism.

The sufficiency of the Bible (Psalm 119:89–104)

Finally, a word needs to be added on the fact that the Bible is a full and sufficient revelation of God. It contains the record of the revelation of Jesus Christ to which nothing can be added, and it is the book which the church has accepted as canonical and as its final authority in all matters of faith. The purpose of biblical interpretation and theology is not to produce new truths which are not in the Bible, but to bring to light the full meaning of what is already contained in the Bible. It is an essential part of Protestant belief that the church can add nothing to the Bible and that all its doctrines must be tested by their fidelity to the Bible.

The Bible is the living voice of God to men. He who inspired the prophets, apostles and holy men to write the Scriptures still speaks through them so that we may come into living contact with Him and receive eternal life. When we read the Bible we seek to hear His Word, and so we pray that the Holy Spirit who inspired its writers may illuminate its readers so that we may know what God is saying to us through it.

REVELATION AND FAITH (1 Corinthians 2)

In this section we have considered four ways in which men learn about God through His revelation of Himself. The question may well be asked, how do we know that these are the ways in which God reveals Himself? What proof is there that they really teach us about God?

The Christian would reply that faith that God is revealed in these ways is one of those great assumptions which are utterly necessary if we are to make sense of the world of our experience. This means that we cannot prove that God exists and reveals Himself to us in the same way as we learn to prove, say, a theorem in geometry. But it does not mean that faith is arbitrary and irrational. On the contrary, there are extremely solid grounds to justify our taking the step of faith in God and in the reliability of His revelation to us; faith in God, like the scientist's faith in the rationality of the universe, is abundantly justified by its results. Our attitude is always one of faith, i.e. of confident trust in the unseen God which passes beyond what the human mind can prove but is not therefore illogical or unreasonable; we find that our faith is confirmed by experience, and we look forward to a day when faith will be replaced by sight.

QUESTIONS FOR DISCUSSION

1. How convincing do you find the so-called 'proofs' for the existence of God to be? If you were attempting to persuade a non-Christian of the existence of God would you begin with them? If not, where would you begin?

2. Can you trace a pattern in God's dealings with Israel from Psalm 78? Do you think that God still acts on the same principles towards the nations of the world?

3. How would you defend the view that the Bible is not merely a record of God's revelation to men in the past but also itself a book which reveals Him to us today?

4. It has been said that the various books of the Bible were accepted by the church into the canon because of their inherent claims to be so accepted: what qualities in the biblical books do you find to be self-authenticating of their divine origin and authority? (It may be helpful to compare some of the books which did not gain admission to the canon; see the 'Apocrypha of the Old Testament' and, for clearer examples, M. R. James, 'The Apocryphal New Testament', Oxford, 1953.)

5. What kind of reliability does the Bible claim for itself? (See the list of references on p. 22.)

6. What would you say is the place of the Old Testament in a book containing the Scriptures of the **Christian** church?

Section 2
THE NATURE OF GOD

The nature and character of God are mysteries and ultimately beyond human understanding. But the fact that He has revealed Himself to us in the ways described in the previous section encourages us to attempt to set out in human words and phrases what may be known about Him. We have to bear in mind continually that these words and phrases are inadequate to express fully the wonder of His character. We ought to regard them as analogies or metaphors which help to tell us what God is like. The reason why these analogies which describe God in human terms can be used with some confidence is that man is a creature made in the image (or 'likeness') of God (Gn. 1:26; see pp. 37 f).

With this caveat in mind about the application of human language to God, we shall now consider, first, the doctrine of the Trinity, and, second, the character of the triune God as love, light and spirit.

THE TRIUNE GOD (Ephesians 1:3–14)

God is revealed to us in the Bible in a threefold way. The Old Testament tells us of **God the Creator and Lord** of the universe. He alone is God, and the idols of the heathen are in no sense gods (Ps. 96:5; Is. 45:12–18). By the time of Jesus the Jews were conspicuous for their strict monotheism (belief that there is only one God; Mk. 12:28–34; Rev. 22:8 f.).

It was in this situation that **Jesus Christ** came among men to reveal God. He claimed to come from God and to share His nature (Mt. 11:27; Jn. 6:38; Phil. 2:6). In this He was unique (Heb. 3:1–6). In certain circles He was described as the 'Logos' or Word of God, a Being separate from God the Father and yet called God (Jn. 1:1; 20:28). He was usually called the Son of God (Acts 9:20; Gal. 2:20); the early church prayed to Him (Acts 7:59 f.; 1 Thes. 3:11 ff.), worshipped Him as Lord (Rom. 10:9–13; cf. Phil. 2:9–11), and, most significantly, applied to Him Old Testament titles of the one God (Phil. 2:10 f., with which compare Rom. 14:10–12 and Is. 45:23; 1 Pet. 2:3, with which compare Ps. 34:8).

Nor was that all. The Old Testament also contained references to the **Spirit of God,** and this Being now came to the fore in New Testament teaching. He was 'another comforter' (i.e. 'strengthener' or 'advocate') sent from God to take the place of Jesus after the ascension and was on an equality with Him (Jn. 14:16 f., 26; 16:7–11, 13–15, 26). He was described as a Person (Rom. 8:26 f.; 15:30; 1 Cor. 12:11; Eph. 4:30; 1 Tim. 4:1) and as divine (2 Cor. 3:17 f.).

The New Testament writers make no attempt to reconcile this teaching about three divine Beings with the Old Testament doctrine of one God. They simply name the three Persons together in a way which suggests irresistibly that they stood on the same level in Christian thought (Mt. 28:19; 2 Cor. 13:14; Eph. 2:18; 4:4–6; 2 Thes. 2:13 f.; 1 Pet. 1:1 f.), although they rarely applied the actual word 'God' to Jesus Christ and less still to the Spirit.

A problem thus faced later Christians. Three independent Persons must surely mean three Gods: how could this be reconciled with belief in the one God? Some early Christians attempted to solve it by regarding the Son and Spirit as lesser, created beings (like the angels) and the Father alone as fully divine; others held that the Three were different 'modes' of existence of the one God, like an actor playing three separate parts in a play, and not separate Persons at all. But neither of these solutions was adequate to explain the beliefs of the biblical writers. Somehow we must maintain that there is one God and that He is Father, Son and Spirit. Four points may be found helpful.

First, while the three Persons, Father, Son and Spirit, are capable of independent action, they are morally at one in thought and purpose, since they are bound to each other by the strongest ties of love and each knows perfectly the mind of the other two (cf. Jn. 5:19 f.; 17:21,23). A husband and wife who are deeply in love and bound together by a single purpose may provide a useful analogy.

Second, it is questionable whether we ought to think of God, Father, Son and Spirit as one collective Person. Very often 'God' really means God the Father. For example, when we pray to God in the name of Jesus (Jn. 16:23) with the Spirit assisting our feeble prayers (Rom. 8:26 f.), we are really praying to God the Father. At the same time, however, the three Persons are united as closely as possible in purpose and action: we may perhaps use the analogy of a political cabinet who are so united in their views that the prime minister can act as spokesman for them all. In other words, when we think of God as a Person, we are usually thinking of the Father, with whom the Son and the Spirit are most closely associated; He is 'God in Three Persons', as a well-known hymn puts it.

Third, various analogies show that the kind of unity implied above is not unprecedented in our ordinary experience. An atom is a unity of various kinds of particles; a biological organism consists of a unity of different indispensable parts; and the human personality unites intelligence, feeling and will in such a way that we can hardly conceive of the whole without its parts nor the parts without the whole. There is nothing impossible in the concept of three Persons united in one God, linked together indissolubly by love without loss of their individual identities.

Fourth, the Son and Spirit are regarded as subordinate to, and in some way dependent upon, the Father as the 'fount' (to use the technical term) of the Godhead. Thus the second Person is called the Son, though we must not infer from this that He had a beginning, but rather that He enjoys a permanent relationship of Sonship to the Father throughout eternity. Again, the third Person is traditionally described as 'proceeding' from the Father and the Son (cf. Jn. 15:26). This does not mean that the three Persons possess varying degrees of divinity, but rather that there is a distinction of function between them in which the Father is supreme.

A final point that should be mentioned is that in the above discussion we have continually used the word 'Person' of each of the three Members of the Godhead. This is a term which has been handed down from some of the earliest theologians in the church, and it must be used with some care. We are able to use it of the Members of the Godhead because they show characteristics which we have come to associate with the idea of human personality. When God revealed Himself to men, He did so supremely through a Person and employed words which are the means used by persons to communicate with each other. But we have to bear in mind that God is greater than men, and that the three Persons of the Godhead are united in a way which is beyond comprehension. Consequently, while the term 'Person' is fully justified in speaking of God, it means more than it does when it is simply applied to men.

THE CHARACTER OF THE TRIUNE GOD

We must now consider the character of God, thinking particularly of the Father, but remembering that the Son and Spirit share the same character and are associated with Him in all that He is and does.

In his Gospel and First Epistle John makes three important affirmations about the nature of God, and we shall use these as the basis of our discussion.

God is love (1 John 4:8)

Love is the character of God from all eternity, for when we ask who is the object of God's love our first answer must be that the three Persons of the Trinity are and always have been bound together by mutual love (Jn. 5:20; Col. 1:13). God's love for the world is, then, an extension of this loving fellowship within the Trinity so as to include the world, and human love is meant to be a copy of this love (1 Jn. 4:11).

In order to understand the nature of this divine love, which is expressed in the Bible by the Greek word 'agapē', we may compare it with the human kind of love which is commonly expressed in Greek by the word 'erōs'. The essence of 'erōs' is a desire to have or possess the object of its love and so to obtain pleasure and satisfaction. It is called forth by the desirableness of its object, it is essentially selfish, aiming primarily at its own good, and its watchword may be said to be 'get'. By contrast, 'agapē' aims to give pleasure and satisfaction to the object of its love. It does not simply love the lovable but reaches to the unlovely and unlovable and makes it lovable. It is fundamentally unselfish and altruistic, aiming at the good of the beloved, and its watchword is 'give'.

It is clear that 'agapē' is the word which alone expresses

the kind of love which God shows. Indeed it derives its meaning from the concept of divine love, since it was only rarely used (and in a colourless sense) before being employed in the Greek translation of the Old Testament. The classical definition of it is found in Paul (Rom. 5:7 f.); it is a love which is concerned with the welfare of the undeserving, conferring benefit on those who showed no love to God. Human love is possibly never free from self-seeking; God's love is given to all men without discrimination and seeks only their highest good.

This, then, is the kind of love which the three Persons of the Godhead show, which led to the creation of the universe, and which brought the Son of God to earth to win back the lost into its joyful fellowship. It is in virtue of such love that God is known as Father, first, of Jesus Christ His Son (Mt. 7:21), second, in a very general sense, of all created beings (cf. Acts 17:28 f.), and, third, in a much more specific sense, of those who have responded to His redeeming love and become His spiritual children (Mt. 6:9,15). In short, love is God's eternal nature.

God is light (1 John 1:5)

In the Bible light is a symbol for such ideas as holiness, goodness, truth, knowledge and salvation; it is a natural name for God who is the supreme embodiment of these qualities (e.g. Ps. 27:1; Mal. 4:2; Jn. 3:19; 8:12; 2 Cor. 6:14; Eph. 5:8 f.; Rev. 22:5).

God is thus revealed to us as holy. Care must be taken not to distinguish this attribute too sharply from His love so as to imply a conflict between the two. Holiness is the moral aspect of God's love. We may say that holiness and love are like the obverse and reverse sides of the same coin. They are both personal attributes of God displayed in personal relationships.

God's holiness may be regarded as His justice, or quality of treating persons fairly. This is not to be understood simply in the law-court sense of punishing the wrong-doer, since it expresses itself primarily in love and mercy even to the undeserving. Thus the gospel itself is a revelation of the righteousness of God (Rom. 1:17): it is precisely because

He is faithful and just that He forgives the penitent sinner (1 Jn. 1:9). He is a righteous God and therefore a Saviour (Is. 45:21). Love is not mere sentiment and justice is not austere payment of what is due. Rather God is both loving and just, and these two aspects of His character are in perfect harmony. True love is justice, and true justice is love.

Because God is holy, He has given men the moral law by which they must live. Love is meant to express itself in harmonious relationships; just as the life of the triune God is marked by perfect harmony, so the life of man in his relationships with his fellow-men and with God should be marked by harmony. The nature of this harmony is revealed to men by God in the divine law which tells them how they ought to live.

The essence of this law is that men ought to love God and each other (Mk. 12:29–31), but it is expanded into a great number of commandments in both the Old and New Testaments. It can be expressed in the form of a command, because holy love itself prescribes a certain way of life; if this way of life is not followed, the fellowship of love is destroyed. The tragedy is that men have refused to acknowledge the demands of God's love expressed in His law. The law of God is unwelcome to them; it is a demand from which they would be free. When love is thus denied the possibility of existence, God's holiness cannot be manifested in any other way than in wrath and judgment.

The reaction of God's holiness to those who refuse to live by His law is His wrath. It is an inevitable consequence of their attitude, since there can be no room in a moral universe governed by the law of love for those who live for themselves without submitting to that law which is part of the structure of the universe. If a man rejects the holy demand and the loving offer of God in His law and gospel, he himself must be rejected and suffer exclusion from the presence of God as a penalty of his rebellion (Mt. 25:31 ff.; 2 Thes. 1:3–12).

Hence God's holiness can be regarded as that which separates sinful men from God. No sinner can stand in His presence where His holiness is visible in all its majesty (Mal. 3:1 f.). It is implied in the Bible that but for their sin men might enjoy fellowship with their Creator (cf. Gn. 2:8; 5:22–24; Ex. 33:11), not, of course, as with a fellow man but with Him who is their Lord and to whom even His own Son is obedient. This fellowship has been destroyed by human sin, and God's holiness has become a barrier to sinners. But God Himself has reopened a way of fellowship through the gospel (1 Jn. 1:3,7). For the righteousness of God not only condemns the sin of the impenitent and separates him from fellowship, but also lovingly seeks to win men back to God, so that by sharing in His holy nature they may renew fellowship with Him (2 Pet. 1:3–11). It is the very wonder of this righteous love which makes the sin of rejecting God the more culpable.

God is spirit (John 4:24)

That God is spirit is probably the most difficult of the three affirmations about Him which we are considering. This is partly due to the great variety of ways in which the word 'spirit' is employed. It is used, for example, of the soul of a man as distinct from his body, or of the life-breath which animates his body, or of the superhuman powers in the world, or of the third Person of the Trinity, the Holy Spirit. Moreover, we find it extremely difficult to conceive what the nature of spirit is, except that it is non-material.

When applied to the Godhead, the word describes the way in which God exists as being basically different from our human bodily existence (cf. Is. 31:3). It guards against thinking falsely of God as having a human or material body like the superhuman figures of Greek gods such as Zeus and Athene. That is why the Bible is so strongly opposed to idolatry and any attempt to make material representations of God (Ex. 20:4–6). Our normal physical and material ways of thinking completely break down when they are applied to God.

The suggestion is also implicit in the use of 'spirit' that God's existence is true, real existence, free from the limitation and the corruption which are associated with bodily existence. In John 4:24 spirit and truth are closely associated. What is spiritual is therefore ultimately real and lasting.

In saying this, we have said very little, and even that little may not be easy to understand. For when we speak of God as spirit, we are in a sense simply confessing our ignorance of the nature of God. We are admitting that there is a realm of reality which we can only vaguely understand. Finite man cannot understand the hidden nature of the infinite God, except through His revelation of Himself in judgment and mercy, and even that revelation contains depths which we cannot fully plumb. For the moment, we can know only in part, but one day we shall know, even as we are known (1 Cor. 13:12). Our task, therefore, is not so much to understand as to worship in spirit and in truth Him who is love and light and spirit.

QUESTIONS FOR DISCUSSION

1. Some modern theologians dislike using the word 'person' in regard to God. Do you think that the teaching of the Bible compels us to retain the use of this word? Are there any dangers to be guarded against in using it?

2. What hints does the Bible give us about the relation of the Father, Son and Holy Spirit to each other? (See the references on pp. 26–29.)

3. On the basis of such a passage as Ephesians 1:3–14, what would you say is the significance of the doctrine of the Trinity for the Christian in his spiritual life?

4. With the aid of a concordance examine the teaching of the New Testament about the Fatherhood of God: what is the significance of the fact that He is rarely said to be the Father of all men?

5. 'The divine attributes of justice and mercy . . . do not need to be reconciled, for they are never at war' (J. Denney): discuss.

6. What place does the law of God occupy in His revelation of Himself to men? How is it related to the gospel, and what is its function in the life of the Christian? (See Galatians 3.)

Section 3

GOD AND THE UNIVERSE

From the study of the intrinsic character of the Godhead we now turn to the relationship which exists between God and the universe. Four aspects of this subject demand our attention. First, we must consider God's **creation** of the universe and His **Lordship** over it. Then we must look more particularly at one of the creatures whom God has made, **man.** and finally we must see how God's relationship to man is affected by **sin.**

CREATION

The teaching of the Bible about creation is remarkably simple. Written in popular, pre-scientific language, it does not give us abstruse, philosophical theories but simple assertions, five of which we may note here.

Creation by God (Genesis 1)

Instead of telling us about the process of creation—which we probably could not understand anyhow—the Bible is content to give us a poetic description of the **fact** that God created the universe. The biblical writer lists what can be seen in the world and asserts that everything owes its origin to God.

This is why the respective tasks of the scientist and the theologian only rarely bring them into collision. The former is concerned with the 'what' of the universe; he tries to give a minute description of it and to explain how it 'works'. The latter is concerned with the 'why' of the universe, i.e. with its ultimate origin, final destiny and moral significance. There is admittedly a 'no man's land' which can belong to either of them, but the work of many scientists who are also Christians shows clearly that the problems in this area are capable of a coherent Christian solution.

Creation out of nothing (Romans 4 : 17)

The authors of pagan myths and early attempts at scientific understanding of the origin of the universe used to think of some kind of previously existing 'stuff' out of which God fashioned the universe, like a potter moulding and shaping a lump of clay. The Bible, however, in the verse mentioned above (cf. Gn. 1 : 1; Heb. 11 : 3) asserts that God's creating work was 'ex nihilo': He created the materials as well as moulding them to shape. We may perhaps go further and say that even space and time were created by God. But it is not easy to think out what that means!

The transcendence of God (Isaiah 40 : 12 ff.)

There is a very old system of philosophy, Pantheism, which teaches that the universe itself is God. It has no support in the Bible, for there we are taught the 'transcendence' of God. God is not to be identified with the universe. He is far greater than that of which He is both Creator and Lord and cannot be bounded by its puny dimensions, even if they are measured in light-years; He inhabits eternity (Is. 57 : 15). This is why the Bible is so vehemently opposed to idolatry, which is the worship of a part of the creation instead of its Creator (Rom. 1 : 25). It is also why the modern criticism of Christianity, that there is no place for God within (or even outside) the universe, is foolish; such a view refuses to reckon with the possibility of other modes of existence than the existence in space and time which is ours.

God's continuing creation (Psalm 104)

Some modern scientists hold the theory that the universe is continually being replenished with supplies of freshly created matter. Whether this theory is true or not, the Bible holds that God's work of creation and care for His universe did not cease after the creation described in Genesis 1. He is not like a watchmaker who, having made and wound up a watch, now leaves it to tick under its own power without any further attention. This is the error which underlies 'deism'. Rather He exercises continual care and control over the universe, and if He did not do so it would simply cease to exist (cf. Col. 1 : 17).

Creation by Jesus Christ (Hebrews 1:1–3)

Jesus Christ is the central figure not only in the new, spiritual creation but also in God's original act of creation. He is not the ultimate Author of the universe—that position is occupied by God the Father—but He is, so to speak, the Agent through whom it was created and He is the One for whom it exists (1 Cor. 8:6). In a similar way, the Spirit of God is associated with the work of creation (Gn. 1:2), so that all three Persons of the Trinity are related to the creation, and the creation exists for their glory.

THE LORD OF THE UNIVERSE

Lordship (Psalm 148)

In the Bible God is described to us not only as the Creator of all things but also as the Lord or Sovereign over all that He has created. His Lordship over creation is usually explained in books on theology by three adjectives which describe His relationship to the creation.

First, God is omnipotent or all-powerful. He is able to do what He wishes to do (cf. Is. 40:21–31). Of course, this does not mean that He is able to do things which are self-contradictory or absurd: we need not rack our brains over the old teaser—'Can God create a stone so heavy that even He cannot lift it?' But it does mean that God is able to do things which transcend human logic and seem impossible to our finite minds, as for example in the incarnation when the Creator Himself became a creature.

Second, God is omniscient or all-knowing. He fully knows and understands the universe which He has created, and nothing which happens in it is hid from His sight (cf. Rom. 11:33–36; Col. 2:3).

Third, God is omnipresent or all-present. It is easy to misunderstand this and to think of God being like some kind of rarified gas or radio waves filling all space. This would be quite misleading. Rather it is implied that no part of the universe is closed from God and His activity. Jacob found that he could not escape from the watchful eye of God by running away from home (Gn. 28:10 ff., especially verse 16), and the psalmist affirmed that it is impossible to flee from

God by day or by night, in life or in death (Ps. 139). Men may find God and commune with Him anywhere and at any time (Mt. 28:20).

It should perhaps be added that the cold sound of these three words may make us think that God's relationship to the universe is cold and abstract. Nothing could be further from the truth. For God shows His character of love and holiness in His dealings with us—a fact expressed when we speak of His providence.

Providence (Psalm 107)

Providence literally means 'foresight' and is a word used in theology to express the idea that God actively cares for His universe and its inhabitants and provides for their needs. Thus the biblical writers ascribed the round of the seasons, the advent of rain and the shining of the sun to God's gracious care for men and His other creatures. They also believed that in some way this care was related to the behaviour of God's people: when Israel was righteous she enjoyed prosperity, but when she served false gods and idols disaster followed (Gn. 1:29 f.; 8:22; Dt. 28; Ps. 104; Mt. 6:25–34; 10:29–31).

The doctrine of providence is not an easy one for the modern mind to grasp. There is certainly not an exact correspondence between human behaviour and divine provision for human needs, and many people find it difficult to reconcile the presence of pain and evil in the universe with the providence of a loving God. Again, it is impossible for us to understand how God causes things to happen. These difficulties are closely related to the problem of evil, which is discussed briefly below, but although no final solution to them can be given, they are not sufficient to overthrow the doctrine of providence. The experience of men and women in the Bible and of Christians in all ages bears witness to Paul's statement that 'in everything God works for good with those who love him' (Rom. 8:28).

THE NATURE OF MAN (Psalm 8)

In the Bible man is the climax and the crown of God's creation. His superiority to all other creatures arises from his being made in the image of God (Gn. 1:26 f.). This phrase means simply that in certain ways man is like, or resembles, his Creator. He has dominion over the world of nature and is able to control his environment and create new things. More important is the fact that he possesses a moral nature. Alone of created beings he is capable of moral behaviour: he knows the difference between right and wrong, between love and hatred. He is capable of fellowship with other men and with God Himself. Hence to say that man is made in the image of God means that he is possessed of a moral and spiritual nature.

Just as the Bible does not try to give us a scientific account of the world in general, so it does not give us a systematic account of the nature of man couched in scientific terminology. It is in fact dangerous to attempt to construct a biblical 'psychology' because the same psychological terms are used in the different books of the Bible with different shades of meaning. In general, however, we can say that in the Old Testament man is regarded as a creature made of flesh and bones; he is described as being (not 'having') a living soul, and his life is inbreathed by God (e.g. 2 Sa. 19:12 f.; Gen. 2:7). In the New Testament, man has a body composed of flesh and blood (1 Cor. 15:50), and he has, or is, a soul ('psychē') and a spirit ('pneuma' (1 Thes. 5:23). Roughly speaking, the word 'body' is used of man as a physical being, 'soul' of him as a being who associates with other men, and 'spirit' of him as a being who has fellowship with God. This is not to say that he has three 'parts': rather, there are three different ways of looking at man.

The purpose of man's existence is, in the classic words of the Westminster Shorter Catechism, 'to glorify God, and to enjoy him for ever'. His life is meant to be centred on God and to be devoted to the praise of God, and he is privileged to enjoy living fellowship with God and with his fellow-men (Eph. 1:12; 1 Cor. 1:9; 1 Jn. 1:3). The Bible teaches quite clearly that men are not meant to live as isolated individuals but in communities, the basic unit of which is the family (cf. Eph. 3:15).

THE MYSTERY OF EVIL

Now that we have looked at the relationship of God and the world without reference to the complicating fact of evil, we must go on to consider how the situation is affected by this factor.

The entry of sin into the world (Genesis 3)

In the biblical narrative the creation of man was soon followed by the entry of evil into his heart. With freedom to choose between right and wrong and between obedience and disobedience, man made the wrong decision at the instigation of the tempter, and sin with all its dreadful consequences entered the world (cf. Rom. 5:12–21; 2 Cor. 11:3).

We should observe that the familiar story in Genesis tells us only the fact of sin's entry into mankind; it does not tell us how or why it happened. Nor does it tell us how the tempter appeared in a world which was 'very good'. There are, it is true, certain passages which suggest some kind of disobedience among angelic beings before the creation of the world (Gn. 6:1–8; Is. 14:12–15; Ezk. 28:12–19; Jude 6), but this simply carries the problem one stage further back and does not explain the origin of evil.

Pain and suffering (Job 24)

There is not only evil in the world in the sense of human wrong-doing. There is also evil in the sense of pain and suffering. Men suffer through the wickedness of their fellow-men, and there are also natural calamities, such as storms and earthquakes, and deadly bacteria and poisons which bring pain and death to men. It cannot always be said that such calamities happen to men in proportion to their own wickedness, and the question, 'Why do the innocent suffer?' is a very real and pressing one.

Various considerations may be urged which lessen the difficulty of this question, but it is impossible for the Christian (or for anybody else) to provide a full and satisfying answer. In evil, pain and suffering we face an ultimate mystery to which there is no solution. The Bible makes it clear that evil is not part of God's plan for the universe, and it is impossible to say that He is responsible for it (Gn. 1:31; Jas. 1:13; such a passage as Is. 45:7 simply asserts that God sends calamity upon men as a penalty for their sins); nevertheless, it is equally clear that we are fallen creatures living in a fallen world. The truth of the matter seems to be that evil is an irrational quantity, a surd, in the universe which God created. The Bible does not explain its origin; it is content to record the far more important facts of God's victory over sin and evil in the cross and resurrection of Jesus and His promise of a new heaven and earth in which pain and sorrow will no longer exist.

The nature of sin (Romans 1:18–32)

Although we can say next to nothing about the origin of sin, we can say quite a lot about how sin works in the hearts of men. We can consider it from three points of view.

In relation to God, sin may be regarded as **rebellion** against Him, expressed in disobedience to His will and laws (Is. 1:2; 63:10; Dt. 17:2; 1 Ki. 8:50), in **falling short** of His standards for human conduct (Lk. 15:18,21; Rom. 3:23), and in worship of other gods, or **idolatry** (Ex. 20:3–6; Lk. 12:13–21; 1 Cor. 10:14–22). Sin is a refusal to accept God as our sovereign Lord, and it results in a perversion of our knowledge of Him (Rom. 1:18–23; 2 Cor. 4:4).

In relation to our fellow-men, sin is expressed in **immorality** (Rom. 1:18-32) and **lack of love** (1 Jn. 3:15; 4:8; Rom. 13:9 f.). A sinner is a person who refuses to respect the rights of other people and disrupts the fellowship of love which is God's purpose for men. He is like a child playing a game who is determined to win at any cost and disobeys the rules in order to beat his competitors.

In relation to oneself, sin is an attitude of **pride** and **self-sufficiency** (Mal. 4:1; Lk. 1:51; Jas. 4:6; 1 Jn. 2:16). It is the attitude of the man who resents any interference from outside in the running of his life, because he is unconcerned about anybody except himself and his own pleasures and because he feels perfectly capable of managing his affairs without taking into account God's law. Sin is self-centred pride.

Sin thus affects every relationship of man, to God, to his

fellows and to himself. Its influence is seen in every part of his life. Its badness corrupts all that he thinks, says and does. This does not mean that he is as bad as he can possibly be, but that no part of him is entirely free from the taint of sin. This is what the theologians call 'total depravity'.

The effects of sin (Romans 2:1–16)

We are mainly concerned in this section with the effects of sin upon men, but it should not be forgotten that sin has cosmic effects. **First,** we may speak of the universe itself as being in some sense 'fallen'. In the Bible natural calamities, hard and unproductive labour, disease, and so on, are all regarded as reflections of the fact that the universe falls far short of the divine pattern for its existence (cf. Gn. 3:14–19; Rom. 8:19–22. But note carefully also Jn. 9:1–3).

A **second** effect of sin is suffering both for the guilty and the innocent. It violates the divine pattern of life, and consequently it shatters man's fellowship with his neighbours, hardens the sinner, cuts him off from communion with God and brings its own consequences in this life quite apart from the final judgment of God (Rom. 1:18–32; Gal. 6:7; Is. 59:2; Rom. 2:5). One of the ugliest features of sin is that it affects not only the individual sinner but also a host of other people who had no part in his particular sin.

A **third** effect of sin is that it enslaves the sinner. Sin is not simply a matter of isolated sinful thoughts and deeds. It is an evil force which enslaves a man in his heart and gains an ever tighter hold upon him so that he becomes more and more incapable of doing the right and the good (Rom. 7:14–20). It is like a cancerous disease which strangles the life out of man.

Fourth, sin leads to guilt in the sight of God. Guilt is not simply a feeling of shame which a man may or may not have after doing what is wrong. It is an objective description of his status in the eyes of the law: a man who breaks the law is objectively guilty, whatever the state of his feelings may be. When a person transgresses God's law, he becomes guilty in the eyes of God and stands under divine condemnation (Rom. 3:19; Jas. 2:10).

Finally, sin leads to death. It is not easy to define death, but we may think of it as the cessation of divine life in a man. Through sin fellowship and contact with God are broken; the sinner fears God's presence (Gn. 3:8; Lk. 5:8; 1 Jn. 2:28); and he passes out of God's care into the power of sin (Rom. 1:24 ff.). Thus a spiritual death of the sinner may be said to take place while he is still physically alive. Physical death itself is symbolic and part of this spiritual death (Gn. 2:16 f.; Rom. 5:12 ff.; 6:23). Finally, the sinner suffers total exclusion from the presence of God; this is spoken of as hell or the second death (Mt. 25:41; 2 Thes. 1:9; Rev. 20:11–15).

Thus the sinner is in a state of death even in this life (Eph. 2:1–5) and stands in desperate need of rescue before his present unhappy state gives way to final condemnation. The doctrine of sin thus poses the question whether rescue is possible and our attention is naturally turned to the second Adam who 'to the fight and to the rescue came'. We must consider the new creation which God has initiated in order to undo the effects of sin in the present world.

QUESTIONS FOR DISCUSSION

1. In what ways is God's continuing activity as Creator and Preserver of the world to be seen?

2. Where do you think points of dispute are likely to arise between science and religion, and what lines of approach would you adopt in attempting to resolve such disputes?

3. What do you think is implied by the biblical teaching that man is made in the image of God? Would you agree that at the fall 'the image was retained (although liable to be defaced and debased)' (T. C. Hammond)?

4. 'Around the explanation of these three passages (Psalm 8:3 f.; Job 7:17 f.; Hebrews 2:6–9), so closely linked, might be gathered no small part of the Biblical doctrine of man' (H. W. Robinson): discuss the question 'What is man?' in the light of these three passages.

5. An old Jewish book states: 'Each of us has been the

Adam of his own soul.' What is your opinion of the truth of this statement in the light of such a passage as Romans 5: 12–21?

6. 'The common notion that sin is selfishness betrays a false assessment of its nature and gravity' (J. Murray). What, then, is the biblical view of the essence of sin?

Section 4
THE PERSON AND WORK OF JESUS CHRIST

The holy love of God for men is supremely revealed to them in the coming of Jesus Christ into the world. God loved the world to such an extent as to become a man in the Person of Jesus in order to save men from their sin (Jn. 3:16; cf. Mk. 10:45; Tit. 2:11). This means that the coming of Jesus is not simply a **revelation** of God's character as holy love: it is an **act** of His love by which He reconciles a sinful world to Himself (2 Cor. 5:19).

We must now consider in detail the way in which Jesus Christ came among men, the work which He performed, and the significance of that work as the means of our salvation from sin.

THE PERSON OF JESUS CHRIST

Jesus Christ as the God-Man (John 1:1–18)

In the New Testament Jesus Christ is revealed to us as being both truly God and truly man. The former of these truths is presented to us in various ways, some of which have been noted (pp. 17, 26 f.), and which are summed up in the titles of 'Son of God' and 'Lord' which were bestowed upon Him.

His true manhood is also attested in various ways. He was made in the likeness of men and of sinful human nature, although He was personally sinless (Rom. 8:3; Phil. 2:7). He had a human mother (Gal. 4:4), and He grew up like any other boy to manhood (Lk. 2:40,52). He experienced the emotions and feelings common to all men—love (Mk. 10:21), sorrow (Jn. 11:33–36), anger (Mk. 3:5; 10:14) and compassion (Mk. 6:34). He knew what it was to be hungry, thirsty and weary (Jn. 4:6 ff.; 19:28). While possessed of supernatural insight and spiritual knowledge, He also had a genuinely human mind and needed to ask questions (Mk. 9:21; 11:13). He felt the need to pray to God (Mk. 1:35;

6:46; Heb. 5:7). He knew what it was to be tempted by the devil beyond measure (Mk. 1:13; 14:32 ff.; Heb. 2:18), but, unlike all other men, He never yielded to temptation (Jn. 8:46; 2 Cor. 5:21; Heb. 4:15; 1 Pet. 2:22).

There is much more evidence than this, but enough has been said to show that the New Testament clearly teaches that the one Person Jesus Christ is to be regarded both as the Son of God and as a real individual man.

Why the Son of God became man (Hebrews 2:9–18)

In the New Testament the doctrines of who Jesus is (His 'Person') and what He does (His 'work') are closely bound up together. Jesus Christ is able to bestow upon us a full salvation only because of the kind of Person that He is. A gift of salvation bestowed by a saviour who was not truly God and truly man would be incomplete and unable to meet the deepest needs of sinners.

It was necessary for Jesus to be truly God. Only the advent of God Himself among men could be a sufficient revelation of His saving love (Jn. 1:14–18), could fully manifest God's intervention to rescue man from his plight (2 Cor. 5:19), and could assure sinners that God wishes them to be adopted into His family as His sons and daughters (Gal. 4:4 f.). Finally, only God Himself could bear the sins of the whole world and atone for them; not even the most perfect of men could do this, for the essence of forgiveness is that the offended person himself (i.e. God in this case) bears the brunt of sin and shows his willingness to forgive, whatever the cost.

At the same time, it was necessary for Jesus to be truly man in order to stand before God on behalf of men and bear the judgment of their sins (Heb. 2:14–18). Only a man could undo the havoc wrought by the first man by becoming a representative of his fellow-men and making atonement for them (Rom. 5:12–21; 1 Cor. 15:21 f.); only with a man can sinners identify themselves in their approach to God (Heb. 4:14 – 5:10).

It was thus necessary for our salvation that God Himself in the Person of His Son should become a man. The doctrine of the 'incarnation' (i.e. that God assumed human flesh) is essential to the Christian doctrine of salvation.

The nature of the incarnate Son of God (Philippians 2:5–11)

The miracle of the Son of God becoming a man is something that hardly permits of human explanation. It is rather like the doctrine of the Trinity, where we found that human language was quite inadequate to explain the mystery of the nature of God as the One in Three. Here we are trying to understand how one person could be both human and divine; and it may safely be said that this also is a mystery beyond our comprehension.

We can, however, make a little progress by looking at false or inadequate understandings of the Person of Jesus Christ which do not do justice to His nature as the God-Man. Many inadequate doctrines of the Person of Christ arose in the days of the early church and still find expression today. We must guard against theories which suggest, for example, that Jesus Christ was a divine Being who only **appeared** to be a man outwardly; or that He was really a man **adopted** by God as His Son; or that He had a kind of **dual personality** with no real union between His divinity and humanity; or that He had a **mixed personality,** being neither God nor man but some kind of intermediate person. Such theories as these fail to do justice to the clear teaching of the New Testament that the Son of God became a man without ceasing to be the Son of God (Jn. 1:14; 2 Cor. 8:9; Phil. 2:5–11). All that we can do is to confess the paradox that Jesus Christ is truly God and truly man, without being able to explain all that this means.

One particular source of difficulty for many people has been to reconcile the possession of divine attributes such as omniscience, omnipresence and omnipotence with the possession of the limited mind and abilities of a man. This has led to a popular theory of the Person of Christ (the 'kenosis' theory) which states that He laid aside or emptied Himself of some of His divine attributes in order to become man, while retaining His love and moral perfection. It is, however, very doubtful whether this theory is really adequate to explain the Person of Christ. It is more likely that it was by the exercise of these very attributes that it was possible for the miracle of incarnation to take place.

The virgin birth of Jesus Christ (Matthew 1; 2; Luke 1; 2)

The coming of Jesus into the world was not like that of an ordinary man, for it was both the birth of a man and the incarnation of the Son of God. Consequently, it is not strange that the mode of His conception and birth was unusual. The New Testament does not deal with this subject very often nor in much detail. Apart from the two narratives of the birth in the Gospels, the New Testament writers are silent on the matter, although there are some indications that they were not ignorant of it (cf. Jn. 1:13; 6:42; 8:41 f.; Gal. 4:4 as possible allusions). This silence is readily explicable during the lifetime of Mary.

The virgin birth, i.e. the fact that the birth of Jesus was the result not of normal human conception but of the special operation of the Holy Spirit (Lk. 1:34 f.), is a miracle, but it need impose no strain on the faith of those who believe in the miracle of the incarnation. The objection sometimes raised to it, that if Jesus was born of a virgin He is not in all things like us (cf. Heb. 2:17), is not really relevant (since this does not affect the reality of His human life from His conception onwards), and the only possible alternative theories, namely that He was the illegitimate son of Mary or the natural son of Joseph and Mary, create far greater difficulties and in any case are not even hinted at in the New Testament (except in such Jewish abuse as that quoted in John 8:41). Only the New Testament doctrine of the virgin birth is adequate as a means of understanding the incarnation of the Son of God.

THE MINISTRY OF JESUS CHRIST

The details of the life and ministry of Jesus are very often omitted from books on Christian doctrine, the tendency being to leap with the Apostles' Creed from 'Born of the Virgin Mary' straight to 'Suffered under Pontius Pilate'. Yet the life of Jesus is important for Christian doctrine, since our doctrine must be based on the historical facts concerning Jesus Christ.

In the space at our disposal there is room only for outlining five major aspects of the ministry of Jesus.

The Proclaimer of the kingship of God (Matthew 4:12–25)

To a world that was under the sway of Satan (Lk. 4:5–7; Jn. 12:31) Jesus proclaimed that God was intervening as King and summoning men to accept Him instead of Satan as their King (Mk. 1:14 f.; Lk. 9:48; 16:13) by becoming His disciples (Mk. 1:16–20) and by obedience to His words (Lk. 6:46 ff.; Mk. 10:14). Those who responded to this summons were taught the new way of life for heirs of the kingdom of God (Mt. 5–7) and sent out to spread the good news that God was beginning to reign through Jesus Christ (Mk. 3:13–15; 5:19; Mt. 28:16–20).

The Ruler of the people of God (Luke 9:18–36)

The preaching of the kingship of God by Jesus fulfilled the Old Testament prophecies (cf. Lk. 4:18–21) of the coming of one who was to usher in the kingdom of God—the Messiah (i.e. an anointed king) to whom the Jews looked for deliverance (Lk. 1:68–79). Thus Pilate's inscription above the cross, 'The King of the Jews', was profoundly true (Jn. 19:19–22).

Jesus, however, avoided the use of the title 'Messiah' because His contemporaries misunderstood its significance. He accepted the title 'Son of David' (Mk. 10:47 f.; 11:9 f.; 12:35–37), but His preference was for the title 'Son of man'. This was taken from Daniel 7 where it describes the representative of the saints of God who, after defeat by their enemies, received power and dominion from God. Thus Jesus was asserting that He was the true Representative and Leader of God's people, that after suffering and rejection He would be vindicated and enthroned by God (Mk. 8:31, 38; 13:24–27; 14:62; Lk. 17:24 f.), and that at the last judgment the decisive factor would be the attitude of men to Himself as the Son of man (Mt. 25:31 ff.; Mk. 8:38; Lk. 12:8 f.).

God's chosen Servant (Luke 22:24–27, 37)

Jesus understood His work as the Son of man in the light of another Old Testament figure, the suffering Servant of God, who is described in Isaiah 40–53. In this prophecy the servant is at first a symbol for Israel, or for the pious minority in Israel, chosen by God to establish justice in the earth and to bring salvation to men (Is. 42:1–7), but as the prophet contemplated the sin of Israel (Is. 42:18–20) he was led to look beyond the nation to an individual servant who would perfectly fulfil the work of God through suffering (Is. 52:13–53:12). There is good reason to suppose that Jesus saw Himself as fulfilling this role as the Servant of God (Mt. 12:18–21; Mk. 10:45; Lk. 22:37).

The Deliverer of sinful men (John 7:53–8:11)

Jesus conceived His work as God's Servant as that of releasing men from the bonds of sin and defeating the prince of this world. In His baptism by John He identified Himself with the sinners whom He came to save (Mt. 3:13–17; cf. Mk. 10:38 f.; Lk. 12:50), and in His death He paid the ransom by which men are released from the power and guilt of sin and enabled to enter the kingdom of God (Mk. 10:45; 14:22–24; Jn. 10:11,17; 12:32). Thus the death of Jesus was the decisive incident in which the kingship of God was revealed in power (Jn. 12:31–33), and His whole ministry, seen as a conflict with sin and evil in every form, was an anticipation of that decisive event (Mt. 4:1–11; Mk. 2:1–3:6; 11:27–12:40; Lk. 11:20).

The Revealer of God (John 14:1–11)

In Jesus, then, we see both the love of God, which gives itself to the uttermost in order to save sinners (Mk. 2:15–17; Lk. 15:1–10), and the judgment of God against all hypocrisy and sin (Mt. 23). As One who loved sinners but warned against sin, Jesus summoned men to accept God as their King, to have their sins forgiven and to enter upon a new life of love (Lk. 5:1–11; 7:36–50). His presence among men was thus an inescapable summons to decision for or against God; it created an hour of crisis in which some responded to the love of God while others refused it (Mk. 4:1–25), an hour in which none could remain unmoved or neutral.

THE DEATH AND EXALTATION OF JESUS CHRIST

The death of Jesus (Mark 14; 15)

No-one can read the story of the death of Jesus Christ without realizing that it was remarkably unlike the death of any other man and that it demands some kind of explanation. It was a death which He accepted willingly, yet only after undergoing deep agony of soul and expressing a desire to avoid it (Mk. 14:36); a death of a kind reserved for criminals, yet He was plainly declared to be innocent of any crime (Lk. 23:13–16); a death under the title of 'The King of the Jews', yet it was the Jews who instigated His death (Jn. 19:19–22).

After it was over, His disciples made the most surprising assertions about it. They claimed that He was the crucified Messiah, an idea completely inconceivable to Jews who believed in a triumphant Messiah (1 Cor. 1:23; note that the Greek 'Christ' is a translation of the Hebrew 'Messiah'); that although wicked men were responsible for His death it was also brought about by the 'determined counsel and foreknowledge of God' (see Acts 2:23); that His death was followed by a resurrection to new and endless life; and, finally, that He who thus died was none other than the Son of God (Gal. 2:20).

We may find a clue to the meaning of this most unusual death in a remarkable cry of the crucified man: 'My God, my God, why hast thou forsaken me?' (Mk. 15:34, quoting Ps. 22:1). The most probable explanation of these words is that Jesus felt Himself to be abandoned by the God whom He usually addressed in the most intimate manner possible as 'Father'. And there would seem to be only one adequate explanation of this experience, namely that Jesus, who was 'reckoned with transgressors' (Lk. 22:37) by His own free choice, was then so closely identified with sinners through bearing the burden of their sin that He felt to the full that exclusion from fellowship with God which is the inevitable consequence of sin (cf. Gal. 3:13).

Further, the unanimous witness of the New Testament is that what Jesus did on the cross He did for us; because of what He has done, we need never suffer that exclusion from the presence of God which is the wages of sin. The only word which is really adequate to describe this role of Jesus Christ on the cross for us is 'substitute', which means that because Jesus in His love has suffered on our behalf we need never suffer the penalty of our sins.

The resurrection of Jesus (Luke 24)

But the story of what God has done for us in Jesus Christ does not end with the cross. There still remained the great act of God the Father in which He set His seal upon the work of His Son, the resurrection.

Into the historical aspect of the resurrection we do not propose to enter here (but see, for instance, Michael Green's 'Man Alive!', Inter-Varsity Press). Our concern is rather with its significance in relation to the death of Jesus, and we may note three points. **First,** the resurrection is a proof of God's justice, in that the innocent sufferer, Jesus Christ, was not allowed to remain unvindicated. The Christian can be confident that He who raised Jesus is the moral Sovereign of the universe, and will similarly vindicate every righteous sufferer who trusts in Him, and bring him into His presence (2 Cor. 4:14).

Second, the resurrection is clear proof that God accepted Christ's finished work on the cross as full and adequate for the salvation of men (Acts 2:32–36).

Third, it is now established that the power of death, both physical and spiritual, is broken for ever. Bodily death is not the final end, for God can raise up men to a new life beyond the grave, and the resurrection of Jesus is the first-fruits or precursor of the resurrection of believers (1 Cor. 15:23). Thus the resurrection is the symbol of Christ's victory over sin and death and the guarantee that He has redeemed us.

The ascension of Jesus Christ (Acts 1:1–11)

But even the resurrection was not the final event in the

earthly life of the Saviour. Forty days after His resurrection Jesus met with His disciples for the last time and, before their eyes, He ascended into heaven. The ascension thus marks the final appearance of Jesus until the day when He shall return in the same way as He departed (Acts 1 : 11; Rev. 1 : 7).

Meanwhile, another Comforter, the invisible Spirit of God, takes His place, so that in a very real sense He still remains with His people and will remain with them until the end of the world (Jn. 14 : 16,18; Mt. 28 : 20). Until that day of His return He sits, according to the symbolism in the New Testament, at the right hand of God the Father (Heb. 1 : 13), having entered heaven as a man (Heb. 4 : 14–16), having presented His finished sacrifice for men to the Father, and having obtained an eternal salvation for men (Heb. 10 : 12–14). His ascension is the symbol that His work of salvation is complete, and He now waits in heaven for the final overthrow of evil (1 Cor. 15 : 25; Heb. 1 : 13).

THE THEOLOGY OF THE CROSS

Such, then, are the facts. We have been unable to relate them without making use of theological language, and we must now consider in greater detail their theological significance as we look at the New Testament teaching about the work of Jesus Christ on the cross for our salvation.

The need for reconciliation between men and God (Ephesians 2 : 1–16)

We have already seen that all men are regarded as sinners in the sight of God. They have chosen to follow sin instead of obeying God, and in consequence of this they have come under the judgment of God, and are liable to death as the result and penalty of their sin, and they have entered into a bondage to evil from which they can find no release.

In this situation three problems surround the provision of salvation for men by God: how can God win men back from love of sin to love of Himself; how can He forgive sinners without condoning sin or denying His implacable opposition to it; and how can He free them from sin so that they may become His willing servants?

This means that there are barriers to be overcome on both the divine and the human sides. God cannot condone sin, and yet seeks some way of restoring sinners to His favour. Man, conscious of his sin, has neither the desire nor the ability to return to God, and fears that he will not be accepted by Him.

The cross is the place where these barriers are broken down; a way is found for God to forgive sin, and a path is opened up for man to return to God by the action of God Himself. In this way an answer is found to the three problems which we have listed.

The cross as revelation (1 John 4:7–12)

The New Testament insists that the atonement (i.e. the act which restores peace between God and sinners and reconciles them to each other) springs from the love of God the Father. The death of Christ was not, therefore, the attempt of one Person of the Trinity to placate an angry Father. Rather, in the death of Jesus we see the supreme revelation of the love of God the Father as He worked through His Son for the salvation of men (Jn. 3:16; Rom. 5:8; Eph. 2:7; Tit. 3:4; 1 Pet. 1:3; 1 Jn. 4:9 f.). It would be completely untrue to say that the Son wrested forgiveness from an unwilling Father.

The cross, therefore, is to be regarded as God's tender appeal to men to return to Him and abandon their sin; it is a demonstration of His love for sinners. Some thinkers have held that this is the deepest meaning of the cross, and that this demonstration of love is an adequate means of atonement between God and sinners. But while there is truth in this suggestion, it cannot be the whole truth. For the love shown at the cross is, above all, **redemptive** love. A mere demonstration of love cannot break the power of evil nor deal with the problem of guilt. The cross shows us love in **action,** actually providing our salvation, and because it is that kind of love it has power to win us back to God.

The cross as sacrifice (Hebrews 9)

In the Old Testament the way in which sinners were restored to a right relationship with God was by the offering of sacrifice. In the case of sacrifices offered for guilt the basic idea was that the sinner confessed his sins to God and offered the sacrificial animal to God who accepted its death, as symbolized in the shedding of its life-blood, as an atonement for sin (Lv. 17:11; Heb. 9:22); God accepted the death of the sacrifice instead of the death of the sinner as an atonement for sin, provided that the sinner repented of his sin. There were, of course, many kinds of sacrifices, some of which did not involve the death of a victim, but the basic view of sacrifice, as understood in the New Testament, was along these lines.

The New Testament regards Christ as fulfilling the function of a sacrifice for men by His death. The sacrificial term 'blood' is used more often than any other expression to indicate the death of Christ (Mk. 14:24; Jn. 6:53–56; Acts 20:28; Rom. 3:25; 5:9; Col. 1:20; Heb. 9:14; 13:11 f.; 1 Jn. 1:7; Rev. 1:5); He is spoken of as a sacrificial Lamb (Jn. 1:29; 1 Pet. 1:19; Rev. 5:6); and His death is regarded as a sacrifice or offering to God (Eph. 5:2; Heb. 10:5 ff.).

In this way, the Old Testament sacrifices are regarded in the New Testament not as efficacious in themselves but as pictures or 'types' of the sacrifice of Christ. They provided the imagery for understanding His death, and at the same time His death was the real basis of forgiveness under the old covenant (Heb. 9:9–14; 10:1–4), being an act with eternal consequences, backwards as well as forwards in time.

Christ, then, died the death which is the result and penalty of sin, and has thus released His people from the need to die that death. He has provided the means by which their sin is 'covered', the wrath of God is 'propitiated' or appeased (though we must always remember that it was God Himself who provided the propitiation; 1 Jn. 4:10), and fellowship between God and men is restored (Rom. 3:25; Heb. 10:19, 20; 1 Jn. 2:2). In this sense we find it necessary to speak of Christ's death as substitutionary and penal, in that He bore to the full the divine reaction against sin on behalf of the race in which He was incorporated. Hence the sinner is able to find salvation as he comes to God in penitence, identifies himself with Christ in submission to the divine judgment, and trusts Christ as his Saviour; he finds that he has to contribute nothing of his own, for Christ has done all that was necessary, and he rejoices in the freedom from condemnation which has become his through the work of Christ, his Substitute (Rom. 5:5–11).

The cross as victory and redemption (Revelation 5:1–14)

Sacrifice is probably the fundamental image for our understanding of the death of Christ, especially where the sinner's relation to God is concerned. When we consider the sinner's relation to sin and its power, however, the idea of the cross as a place of victory and redemption becomes important.

From this point of view, the cross is seen as the culmination of Christ's conflict against sin and Satan in His ministry (Jn. 12:31; Lk. 10:17–19). Put very simply, the cross was the attempt of wicked men inspired by the power of evil to put a stop to the ministry of Christ. But it was a complete failure! He rose from the dead, and His ministry still continues. Satan was unable to tempt Jesus to sin during His ministry or to make Him yield to the power of death. On the contrary, the New Testament speaks of the cross as the place where Satan was judged and defeated, so that he is now a defeated foe whose final doom is sealed. He and his minions can no longer lord it over those who trust in Christ, for Christ is even now enthroned as Lord (Eph. 1:20 f.; Phil. 2:9–11; Col. 2:15; Heb. 2:14 f.; 1 Pet. 3:22).

With this idea is connected the thought that the death of Christ is the means of redeeming men from the power of sin. In the Old Testament the idea of redemption was used to express God's mighty acts of deliverance for His people (e.g. the Exodus from Egypt). The tremendous cost of such deliverance is the point of emphasis, rather than any idea of payment made to somebody (Ex. 6:6; Ne. 1:10; Pss. 77:14 f.; 130:8; Is. 43:1–4; 63:9; Je. 50:34). The death of Christ is seen as the culmination of God's great acts of deliverance in the past whereby He chose and rescued a people for Himself (Lk. 1:68; 24:21; Tit. 2:14). The legal ceremony in which a slave was freed on payment of a ransom price was probably also in Paul's mind when he spoke of redemption (1 Cor. 6:20; 7:23; cf. Rom. 3:24; Gal. 4:5; 2 Pet. 2:1). Christ has thus delivered men from sin at tremendous cost

(Eph. 1:7; 1 Pet. 1:18) so that they may become the willing slaves of God (1 Cor. 7:22 f.), and they now look forward to the day when Satan is brought into final captivity and they enter into the full joy of their final redemption (Lk. 21:28; Rom. 8:23; Eph. 4:30).

QUESTIONS FOR DISCUSSION

1. 'Veiled in flesh the Godhead see' (Charles Wesley): do you find this to be a satisfactory definition of the incarnation?

2. What important truths about the Person of Jesus Christ are safeguarded and expressed in the New Testament narratives of the virgin birth?

3. What evidence can you gather from the first three Gospels to show that entry to the kingdom of God depends upon a man's personal attitude to Jesus Christ? (A concordance will probably be found useful here.)

4. 'If Christ had done less than die for us, there would have been no atonement' (J. Denney): why not?

5. What significance is attached to the concept of the blood of Jesus in the New Testament? (See the references on p. 54.)

6. 'If Christ has not been raised, your faith is futile and you are still in your sins' (1 Cor. 15:17): would anything be left of Christianity if the resurrection had not taken place?

Section 5
THE LIFE OF THE CHRISTIAN

We have now seen the state of men as sinners in the sight of God and the way in which Jesus Christ has come to be their Saviour. We must next consider the new life which He bestows upon those who accept Him as their Saviour from sin. First of all we shall look at two general words which are used to describe our experience as Christians; second, we shall discuss four different aspects of the Christian life; and, third, we shall consider our response to God's gift of salvation and new life.

Salvation (1 Peter 1:3–12)

Salvation is probably the most general term used in the Bible for the great gift which men receive by believing in Jesus Christ (Rom. 1:16).

We find that the verb 'to save' or 'to be saved' is used in all three tenses. Christians are people who **have been** saved: the time when they first put their trust in Jesus Christ marks the beginning of their experience of salvation (Eph. 2:5,8). They are people who daily **are being** saved as they continually experience more and more of the love of Christ and increase in faith and knowledge (2 Cor. 2:15; cf. Eph. 3:14 ff.). But their salvation is not yet fully given to them, so that the Bible can speak of it as a future gift: they **will be** saved in the day of God's final triumph (2 Tim. 4:18), and thus they now live in hope of that future salvation (Rom. 8:24).

These three tenses of salvation are put alongside each other in 1 Peter 1:3–5, and the explanation of them is that Christians believe in One who is able to save 'to the uttermost' (Heb. 7:25, AV; literally 'for all time') those who come to God by Him. His name 'Jesus' means 'Saviour' (Mt. 1:21). Such salvation is both negative and positive. It is a salvation **from** sin and the wrath of God (1 Tim. 1:15; Rom. 5:9), and it brings us **into** knowledge of God (1 Tim. 2:4). Finally, it is from first to last given to us by God's gracious act in Jesus Christ (Acts 15:11) and received by faith in Him (Rom. 10:5–17).

Eternal life (John 6:27–71)

A second way of describing God's gift of salvation is as life, or as eternal life. The idea here is that sinners can properly be regarded as dead while they live in this world and are destined for eternal death in the next world (Eph. 2:1–5; Rom. 6:23); but the coming of Jesus has brought true life to men (2 Tim. 1:10). Thus Christians are assured that the grave is not the termination of life but the gateway into everlasting life in the presence of God and of Christ (Jn. 5:29; 11:23).

This life is 'eternal' not only in 'length' but also in 'depth'; it is called 'eternal' not simply because it is everlasting, but primarily because it is a sharing in the life of God Himself (Jn. 5:25 f.; 2 Cor. 4:10 f.); eternal life is in fact defined as the experience of knowing God (Jn. 17:3)—an experience which is beyond the ken of the sinner (Eph. 4:17 f.).

The great fact emphasized in the New Testament is that eternal life is not simply a hope of new life beyond the grave; it is the present possession of every Christian here and now in this world (Jn. 5:24; 6:47). The present life of the Christian is a foretaste of the life of heaven; here and now we know God and experience His love (1 Tim. 4:8; Jn. 11:25 f.; 1 Jn. 3:14; 5:11). Even though our bodies outwardly perish, our 'inner man' possesses the life of God (2 Cor. 4:16), and we shall in the end openly possess that life which is now our hidden possession in Jesus Christ (Col. 3:3 f.). Until that day we draw continual sustenance from Him and receive His pledge of immortality (Jn. 6:35,54).

PEACE WITH GOD

We shall now consider four ways in which we experience God's gift of salvation and eternal life. The first of these aspects of salvation is our new relationship of peace with God and we shall discuss it with the aid of three key words.

Justification (Romans 3:20–31)

Justification is the word used by Paul to describe the gracious act of God in pardoning and receiving sinners. It is a legal term and refers to the action of a judge in declaring a man who is on trial to be innocent. In the Old Testament stern warnings are addressed to human judges who justify or acquit evil and ungodly men (Pr. 17:15); in the New Testament God Himself justifies or acquits the ungodly and the sinner (Rom. 5:8 f.).

How can this be possible? Paul answers that justification or acquittal springs from the grace of God and rests on the fact that Jesus Christ came to be the sacrifice or propitiation for human sin (Rom. 3:24 f.). He came and lived a perfect life of obedience to God; He identified Himself with sinners and their sin, and on their behalf and in their place He submitted to the just claims of the law of God and bore its curse (2 Cor. 5:21; Gal. 3:13). Because of His perfect obedience and righteousness, those who make themselves one with Him by faith are reckoned by God as righteous, not because of any merit of their own but because they trust in Christ alone as their righteousness (Rom. 4:20–25; 1 Cor. 1:30).

Thus those who admit their sinfulness before God and put their trust in Christ find that they no longer have to receive the wages of their sin but are freely acquitted or justified by God for the sake of Christ. Because of what He has done, sinners no longer need to try to do good works as a means of pleasing God and winning salvation (Rom. 4:5; Eph. 2:8–10). Nevertheless, true faith in God will express itself in good works: good works are the **fruit** of justification, but not its **cause.**

Forgiveness (Luke 7:36–50)

Justification is, as we have seen, originally a legal word, but in the New Testament its meaning is transformed through its link with God's grace. Forgiveness is a word that refers to personal relationships. It expresses the same truth as justification, but it does so from a more personal point of view (Rom. 4:7).

The New Testament speaks much of the forgiveness of sins as the great blessing which God bestows upon Christians. Jesus Christ came to declare God's forgiveness to men (Lk. 7:48) and His death upon the cross is the means by which forgiveness is extended to us (Mt. 26:28; Eph. 1:7). Thus the way to receive divine forgiveness is through faith in Him (Acts 10:43).

Justification is an act which can be performed only by God as the sovereign Judge. But forgiveness is an act which can be performed by men. So those who receive free and unmerited divine forgiveness are to be equally ready to forgive others (Mt. 6:14 f.; Eph. 4:32). Further, while justification is usually regarded as a single act of God (anticipating His verdict on the day of judgment), forgiveness can be regarded as something for which we pray daily (Mt. 6:12; 1 Jn. 1:9); for the justified sinner is still prone to sin and he needs to seek forgiveness daily from his heavenly Father.

Reconciliation (2 Corinthians 5:14–21)

The result of divine justification and forgiveness is that the sinner has peace with God (Rom. 5:1) and with his fellow Christians (Eph. 2:14 f.). This restoration of peace and friendly relations is called reconciliation. The New Testament teaches that men do not need to do anything to reconcile God and make Him their friend; rather He Himself has in His grace carried out the great act of reconciliation in Jesus Christ, thus making it possible for sinners to be reconciled to Him, and He summons them through the preachers of the gospel to accept the reconciliation which He has provided for them by the sacrifice of Jesus Christ (2 Cor. 5:18–20; Rom. 5:10 f.).

In this way full harmony is restored between sinful men and their God. He Himself justifies, forgives and reconciles them; He no longer reckons their sin against them, but gives them a new status in His sight. It is true that they may still sin against Him and continually need to seek forgiveness and cleansing; they are at one and the same time justified and yet still sinners; but because they trust in Christ for their salvation they need no longer fear the wrath of God.

SONS OF GOD

Those who have been justified and forgiven by God have a new status in the sight of God. They now become heirs of eternal life (Tit. 3:7). They are members of the family of God and inherit all the blessings that come to His children.

Conversion (Matthew 18:1–4)

The act of coming into the new relationship of peace with God by faith in Jesus Christ is such a decisive and far-reaching one that the New Testament sometimes speaks of it as conversion. Men are summoned by God to a complete 'right-about turn' in their way of life: they must turn from their old ways and seek after God (1 Thes. 1:9 f.). They must be ready for the humiliating step of becoming like helpless children who cannot do anything for themselves but must trust in the care of their parents. From a human point of view, therefore, to become a Christian involves an act of conversion in which we become dependent like little children. From the divine point of view this is true in a deeper sense, because God actually makes us His children.

The new birth (John 3:1–17)

Two very similar metaphors are used in the New Testament to describe the way in which men become children of God. According to the first of these, men undergo an experience which can be described as a new or spiritual birth. Conversion is a change of such magnitude, involving the reception of eternal life, that it can be compared only to the act of birth (cf. Mt. 18:3). This new birth is the work of God Himself who puts the seed of a new divine life within us through His Word and His Spirit (Jn. 3:5; 1 Pet. 1:23) when we believe in Jesus Christ (Jn. 1:12 f.; 1 Jn. 5:1) who died to bring us life (Jn. 3:14 f.). In this way we enter upon a new life as the children of God (Jn. 1:12 f.), characterized by hope (1 Pet. 1:3), righteousness (1 Jn. 3:9) and love (1 Jn. 5:2).

Adoption (Galatians 4:1–7)

The other metaphor used to describe the way in which we become sons of God is that of adoption. The Christian is a person who once was not a member of God's family but now has been adopted into it with the full privileges of a son. This is because Christ has redeemed him from sin. When he puts his trust in Christ, and is thus 'united' with Christ, he becomes by adoption what Christ is by nature (Rom. 8:17). Another way of putting this is to say that we receive the Spirit of God (Rom. 8:14), just as Christ Himself possessed the Spirit of God (Lk. 3:22); it is because we possess the Spirit that we feel constrained to call God 'our Father' (Rom. 8:15).

Sons of the Father (Matthew 6:24–34)

In this way, then, Christians have the right to call God their Father, and He for His part cares for them and freely bestows His love upon them. It is not generally realized that the Bible very rarely speaks of God as the Father of all men. While He is certainly the Father of all men as their Creator and Preserver, the Bible usually keeps the word 'Father' for the special relationship which He has towards those who love and fear Him and have been adopted into His family. Those who are His children in this sense are meant to show the 'family likeness' by living lives of holiness and love (Lk. 6:36; 1 Pet. 1:15–17), and they are disciplined by Him so that they may become more holy (Heb. 12:5–11).

PARTAKERS OF CHRIST

Christians are not only specially related to God as His sons; they have also a special relationship with Jesus Christ and with the Holy Spirit. It is, of course, impossible rigidly to distinguish between these relationships with the different Persons of the Trinity, since they all work together for our salvation; nevertheless we may here consider the way in which Christians are particularly related to their Saviour.

In Christ (John 15:1–11)

The basic relationship of the Christian to Jesus Christ is, as we shall discuss presently, an attitude of faith and trust. By such faith the Christian is closely united with his

Saviour. Thus the Christian can be described as a member of the body of Christ (1 Cor. 12:27); he has been baptized into the name of Christ (Acts 8:16) or simply into Christ (Rom. 6:3), and can be said to have 'put on Christ' (Gal. 3:27). So close is this union that the Christian can be said to be 'in Christ', a phrase which is used by Paul at least 160 times, with various shades of meaning (2 Cor. 5:17; Gal. 3:28; Eph. 1:1; Phil. 1:1, et al.); at the same time it is equally true to say that Christ is in the Christian (Rom. 8:10; Col. 1:27). Jesus uses the same idea when He says that He abides in the believer and the believer abides in Him (Jn. 15:4–7).

In this way it is shown that the Christian is united with Jesus Christ by faith. Or we may say that the Christian lives a new life as a member of the body of Christ, drawing his strength from the Head and acting as the agent of the Head in the world. A new and vital union has been set up between the believer and his Lord in virtue of which the believer receives the power of Christ and is commissioned for the service of Christ.

Identification with Christ (Romans 6)

In particular, the believer shares in the experiences of Christ, so that the pattern of Christ's life becomes the pattern of his life. We have already seen that Jesus Christ died and rose **for** us; we must now learn the further truth that we die and rise **with** Christ.

When Jesus Christ died on the cross, He died for all men, so that it is also true to say that all men died in Him (2 Cor. 5:14). But the death which He died was a death to sin; that is to say, by dying He passed out of the dominion of sin, for sin can have no power over or claims upon a man who is dead. This means that Christians who have died with Christ, a fact symbolized by the rite of baptism in water, are no longer under the dominion of sin; it need no longer be their master (Rom. 6:3,6,7). Their old selfish nature, which was the seat of sin, has been crucified with Christ, and they do not live to serve their selfish desires any longer.

Similarly, when Jesus Christ rose from the dead, all believers rose with Him (Rom. 6:4 f.). By resurrection He entered upon a new life in the power of God. Consequently, Christians who rise with Him, a fact symbolized again by the rite of Christian baptism, enter upon a new life empowered by God, with service to God as their single purpose (Rom. 6:4,8–11).

This identification with Christ, whereby believers die to sin and live to God, takes place at the time of conversion but needs to be sustained by a continual attitude of faith in Christ. Moreover, it is a fact of unhappy experience that sin and temptation still torment the person who is identified with Christ, and therefore Paul exhorts Christians to persist in faith and to believe that Christ is able to communicate new life to them and enable them to overcome the old sinful nature. The Christian life is a battle, but a battle in which victory is possible because the power of God is available to the Christian, so that day by day he can win fresh victories over the power of sin.

Thus, although the Christian may at times see outward defeat and decay in his life, he is to continue in belief, in the sure hope that he who suffers with Christ will also reign with Him (2 Tim. 2:11–13). As one who has been crucified with Christ, he is to live by faith in Christ (Gal. 2:20) with the assurance that one day he will share in the resurrection glory of Christ which he has now begun to know in part (2 Cor. 4:10–14).

POSSESSORS OF THE SPIRIT

Our fourth way of looking at the Christian life is as possession of the Spirit of God. It is through the work of God's Spirit in our hearts that we are born again and adopted into the family of God. He is also described as the Spirit of Christ, so that it does not greatly matter whether we speak of Christ or of the Spirit indwelling our hearts (Rom. 8:9–11). We may think of Him as the One who applies salvation to us and fills us with the power and blessing of God.

The Spirit of holiness (Romans 8:1–17)

In the Bible the Spirit of God is most frequently spoken of as the Holy Spirit. It is by His work in the heart that the

Christian becomes holy (2 Thes. 2:13), i.e. begins to share in the loving and righteous character of God. The Spirit takes possession of a man when he believes in Christ (Rom. 8:15), confirms his faith (Rom. 8:16), and strengthens him to live the Christian life (Eph. 3:16; 2 Tim. 1:7).

The name given to those who possess the Spirit of 'holiness' is 'saints' (the two words are translations of the same Greek root); indeed this is one of the most characteristic names for God's people. The word 'saint' carries two closely allied meanings. First, it refers to those who are consecrated to God's service and belong to Him. It is because of this that all Christians, no matter how unholy they may sometimes be, are called saints (cf. 1 Cor. 1:2—addressed to a church which was by no means perfect in holiness). Second, it refers to those who are holy and share the character of the God to whom they belong; thus saints are called to live in a manner worthy of God, and this is possible by the sanctifying power of the Spirit.

The fruit of the Spirit (Galatians 5:16–26)

As a person who is called to be a saint and in whom the Spirit dwells, the Christian is commanded to live no longer according to the old principle of sin (referred to by Paul as 'the flesh'), but according to the new principle of the Spirit, which empowers him to fulfil God's law of love (Rom. 8:1–4). Since he possesses the Spirit, he is to submit to the guidance of the Spirit, to put to death his sinful nature, and to allow the fruit of Christian character to grow in him. In the power of the Spirit he need no longer produce the fruit of a sinful life; rather his joy and delight will be to abound in the kind of life which is inspired by the Spirit of God.

The assurance of the Spirit (Romans 8:14–16)

Such life according to the principle of the Spirit is one of the surest signs that we are Christians. It is one of the ways in which the Spirit convinces us that we are truly God's children who will one day receive our full inheritance. Even now the Spirit is gradually transforming us, so that one day we will be completely holy (1 Thes. 5:23). Thus the possession of the Spirit is at once the mark or seal of God's ownership stamped upon us, and the first taste of the full blessing which will be ours in the day of our full salvation (2 Cor. 1:22; 5:5; Eph. 1:13 f.).

THE HUMAN RESPONSE

Such, then, is the Christian life viewed as the gift of salvation and new life bestowed upon us by the grace of God. Our task is now to consider the nature of the response which we must make to God and the way in which we receive the blessings of salvation.

Faith (Romans 10:1–17)

Christian salvation is from first to last the free gift of God's grace to men. There is, therefore, nothing that men can do to earn salvation or to make themselves worthy of receiving the gift. If that were possible, it would mean that the work of Jesus Christ was incomplete and that He had died to no purpose (Gal. 2:21). This means that faith, which is the biblical word for the human response to God's grace, is simply the holding out of our hands to receive the divine gift. There is nothing to do, except to receive what God graciously offers to us.

Faith is thus essentially an act of acceptance of what God offers to us. But this means that it must also include an attitude of belief in the promises of God. A person who comes to God must believe that He exists and rewards those who seek Him (Heb. 11:6); he must have some belief, however elementary, that Jesus is able to save him before he can receive salvation, even if he feels constrained to pray for greater faith (Mk. 9:24). Thus faith is an act of trust in the unseen God, based on what He has revealed of Himself in the Scriptures which bear witness to His great act of salvation in Jesus Christ.

Two further elements must be mentioned which are also essential aspects of this basic attitude of trust in God.

Repentance (Luke 19:1–10)

Negatively, Christian faith is a turning away from sin and evil. A true faith in God is measured by a man's willingness to leave behind the sins and false gods which have filled his life and to allow God to rule over him. The very demons, says James, believe in God and tremble, but that is not enough to save them (Jas. 2 : 19). To be a Christian involves realizing that our sin has hurt God and being sorry that we have grieved Him. There must be a readiness to give up sin and all that God hates. This, of course, is not a 'work' which we do in order to placate God; rather it is the response of our love to Him who first loved us.

Consecration (Colossians 3 : 1–17)

Positively, Christian faith is characterized by total submission to God in Christ. A Christian is a man who has turned from idols to serve God (1 Thes. 1 : 9); he has yielded his whole self to God so that he may be perfected in holiness (Rom. 6 : 13,16–23). He regards Jesus not simply as a Saviour but also as a Lord to be obeyed. For God has called him to a full salvation, and this salvation can never be complete so long as any part of his life is not yielded to God.

Both repentance and consecration are to be regarded not simply as once-for-all acts by which we become Christians, but as new and continual attitudes of the believer. We normally employ the word 'conversion' to signify the initial decisive change by which a person becomes a Christian, but a Christian needs also to undergo a process of 'continuous conversion' involving daily repentance and consecration as long as he remains in this sinful world and is subject to sin and temptation.

Thus Christian faith is a lifelong attitude to God; it means grateful acceptance of all that God has done for us, and it is characterized by three elements—trust in God's promises, abandonment of all that God hates, and entire committal to Him.

Finally, faith finds expression in prayer and good works.

Prayer (Luke 11 : 1–13)

Through prayer we express our faith in God. In it we draw near to Him and praise and adore Him for all His goodness to us; we express our trust in Him by making our petitions to Him and believing that He will answer them according to what is best for us. We express our consecration by praying 'Thy will be done'. Our prayers are made in the name of Jesus, since it is through Him that we have bold confidence to approach God's 'throne of grace' (Heb. 4:14–16), and the Holy Spirit of God Himself assists us in our prayers (Rom. 8:26 f.).

Good works (James 2:14–26)

If faith is expressed towards God in prayer, it finds expression as regards our fellow-men in good works. The Christian has been saved not for his own sake alone but in order that he may do good (Eph. 2:10). While it is true that good works cannot save a man, nevertheless true faith will inevitably find expression in good works of love and mercy, and a faith which does not issue in good works is not faith at all (Jas. 2:26). Thus Paul speaks of 'faith working through love' (Gal. 5:6). And John says that the man who claims to love God but hates his brother is a liar (1 Jn. 4:20).

This serves to remind us that faith and the Christian life are not simply a matter of individual relationship with God, and leads us on to consider the life of the Christian as a member of the people of God in the church.

QUESTIONS FOR DISCUSSION

1. What aspects of salvation, past, present and future, can you discover from a study of 1 Peter 1:3–9?

2. What grounds has a Christian for being sure that he has been saved and that he will enter into the life of heaven?

3. What relationship would you say exists between justification and sanctification in the life of the believer?

4. How is holiness expressed in practice in the life of the Christian? (Such a passage as Ephesians 4:17–32 will form a useful basis for study.)

5. 'The man who would know how central the Spirit is to Paul's Christianity should ponder well Galatians 5, 2 Corinthians 3 and Romans 8, not forgetting 1 Corinthians 12–

14, which treat of the Spirit's gifts' (A. M. Hunter): examine any of these passages in order to discover the place of the Spirit in the life of the Christian.

6. What does the New Testament teach about the value of 'good works' done (a) before and (b) after conversion?

Section 6
THE CHRISTIAN COMMUNITY

Our theme in this section is the Christian doctrine of the church. It is important to observe from the very outset that this subject is not an optional extra only vaguely related to the subject of our previous chapter. Rather, the two subjects are inextricably linked together, because a man cannot become a Christian by faith in Jesus Christ without at the same time becoming a member of the people of God along with all his fellow-believers and sharing in the life of the church (1 Cor. 1 : 26). Jesus did not come to save individuals in isolation from each other but to found a new community of Christians who would build each other up in the faith and through whom His purpose for the world would be accomplished. Let us then consider in greater detail what it means to be a Christian in God's new community.

THE NATURE OF THE CHURCH

Under this heading we shall consider the purpose of Jesus in His ministry and the various ways (nearly all of them derived from the Old Testament) in which the church is described as the people of God in the New Testament.

Jesus and the church (Matthew 16 : 13–28)

If there is one phrase which Jesus used more than any other in His teaching it is 'the kingdom [literally, 'kingship'] of God' (Mk. 1 : 14 f.). He came to teach men that in Him God stood among men as their King and summoned them to accept Him as their King. This can only mean that Jesus came to gather together a company of people who accepted God as their King.

In making this His message, Jesus was not preaching anything new. For the Old Testament is the story of how God chose the nation of Israel that they might be His people and He might be their God (1 Sa. 12 : 12). But the Old Testament is also the story of how Israel time and time again refused to accept God as their King (1 Sa. 8:7). When Jesus came, He made a final appeal to Israel, but by and large He was rejected by them. So He turned to His company of twelve disciples and announced that the kingdom was to be given to them and not to disobedient Israel; His disciples were to be the nucleus of a new Israel, the church of God (Mt. 21:43; 16:18; Lk. 12:32). Thus the church is to be understood as the new Israel who accept God as their King and Jesus as the Messiah (or Christ). Entry to the church is by becoming a disciple of Jesus and accepting God as King.

When, then, was the church founded? It existed in the Old Testament (Acts 7:38), and we may see its beginnings anew in the company of Jesus' disciples. But it is probably best to see its real beginning on the Day of Pentecost; it was only then that the kingdom of God had been manifested in power by the victory of Jesus on the cross (cf. Rom. 1:4); on that day the Holy Spirit was first given to Christians (Jn. 7:39).

The names of the church (see references below)

One of the best ways to understand the nature of the church is to consider the names used for it in the New Testament. We have already considered some of these, but may rapidly recapitulate them.

First, the Church is the true or spiritual Israel of God. The word **church** (Gk. 'ekklēsia') is found in the Greek version of the Old Testament to mean the assembly (the AV has 'congregation') of God's people. Christians are regarded as the **people** of God, and the significant thing is that this people includes the Gentiles who believe in Christ (Acts 15:14; Rom. 9:24–26; 2 Cor. 6:16; Tit. 2:14; 1 Pet. 2:9 f.). They are described as the **Israel** of God (Gal. 6:16; Eph. 2:12,19). They are the **flock** of God, and He is their Shepherd (Lk. 12:32; Jn. 10:1–16, 26–29; Acts 20:28; 1 Pet. 5:3). They are the **bride** of Christ, just as the old Israel was the bride of Jehovah (2 Cor. 11:2; Eph. 5:22 ff.).

Second, the church is the dwelling of God on earth. Just as individual Christians are spoken of as temples of the Holy Spirit (1 Cor. 6:19), so the church as a whole is the **temple** or dwelling-place of God (1 Cor. 3:16 f.; Eph. 2: 19–22). In the same way, the church is a **building** which is being constructed by God (1 Cor. 3:9; Eph. 2:19 f.; 1 Pet. 2:5), or a **household** (Gal. 6:10).

Third, the church is the **body** of Christ (Rom. 12:4 f.; 1 Cor. 12:2 ff.; Eph. 1:22 f.; 4:4,12,15 f.; 5:23). This is a phrase especially loved by Paul, and by it he means that the church is composed of various members united to each other and to Christ as their Head in the closest possible manner, like the various parts of the human body.

In these various ways it is clearly taught that the church is a unity of members with Christ as their Head and God as their King. We must now look at its purpose and work in relation to God, itself and the world.

THE LIFE OF THE CHURCH

Worship (1 Peter 2:1–10)

The church is first and foremost a company of people who owe allegiance to God and His Son, Jesus Christ. This means that its primary function is to worship and glorify God; the church is most truly the church when its members are gathered together to worship God.

In the Old Testament the people of Israel are described as a kingdom of priests (Ex. 19:6) whose function it was to offer sacrifices of praise and thanksgiving to God. Similarly, in the New Testament the church is a royal priesthood to offer praise and thanksgiving to God (1 Pet. 2:5,9). This does not, of course, mean that the church is to offer sacrifices to God for sin; that has been offered once and for all by Christ (Heb. 9:24–28). Rather we are to serve God by praising Him for His goodness (Heb. 13:15; Rev. 5:11–14; 7:9–12), by putting our lives at His disposal (Rom. 12:1), and by performing good works (Heb. 13:16).

Fellowship (1 John 1:1–7)

The word 'fellowship' means the sharing of several people in a common possession, and it expresses the main idea used in the New Testament to describe the life of the church. The church is a company of people who have one King and who share together in one gift of salvation in Jesus Christ (Jude 3; Tit. 1:4). Although its members may be different in age, sex, race, colour, wealth, social status and ability, they are joined together as one people (Gal. 3:28; 1 Cor. 12:13; Col. 3:11), sharing in the gift of the one Spirit (Eph. 4:3 f.; Phil. 2:1), and exercising mutual generosity as regards their material possessions (Acts 2:44; 4:32). As Christ's disciples, they are called to share with Him in suffering for the sake of the gospel (Phil. 3:10; Rev. 1:9) and are promised a share in His glory and kingly rule (2 Tim. 2:12). In this way there is an intimate union between God, Christ and all Christians through the Spirit (1 Cor. 1:9; 2 Cor. 13:14; 1 Jn. 1:3–7).

From this fact follow two inescapable consequences. **First**, the life of those who share in the fellowship of God's people is to be characterized by love. We have already spoken of the quality of God's love which is not motivated by selfish gain but loves to give freely without any partiality. Christians are to love each other in that spirit, since that is how Christ loves them (1 Jn. 4:7,11; Eph. 5:2). Christian love is the 'greatest thing in the world' (see 1 Cor. 13). So the essence of Christian ethics is the command to love one another. It is summed up in the golden rule: 'Whatever you wish that men would do to you, do so to them' (Mt. 7:12). Such love is, of course, not confined to members of the Christian fellowship, but is to extend to all men (Lk. 10: 25–37; Gal. 6:10).

Second, the church is to be a unity. The New Testament knows of only one church, since Christ cannot be shared out among competing and rival groups of Christians (1 Cor. 1: 10,13). Since, therefore, there is but one church which finds its outward expression in local groups of believers, each of which can be called the church, it follows inescapably that such local churches ought to exist side by side in love and harmony. Church divisions in the New Testament are geographical, not based on difference of doctrine or practice. Our modern concept of 'denominations' is quite foreign to the New Testament. All Christians, therefore, ought to love and serve one another, and all churches similarly ought to love and serve each other.

This does not necessarily mean that all local churches will

do everything in exactly the same way; it does mean that all churches should love each other and strive together to glorify God. It is, however, sadly possible for churches as well as individual Christians to fall into error and sin, and in such cases it is the duty of the Christian to speak the truth in love and seek to restore the unity of faith which has been disrupted. In extreme cases, drastic measures may become necessary (e.g. Gal. 1:8), as at the Reformation, but these are only to be contemplated when other means of restoring truth, love and unity in the church have failed.

Witness (Matthew 28:16–20)

The task of the church as regards the world is to carry on the ministry of Jesus Christ. As He was sent by His Father to bring salvation to men, so He sent and still sends His church to do His work in the world (Jn. 17:18,20). For this purpose the church is given the power of the Holy Spirit, who is especially at work whenever the gospel of Christ is preached (Rom. 15:18 f.; 1 Thes. 1:5; 1 Cor. 2:4; 2 Cor. 6:6).

The preaching of the gospel to the Gentiles is part of the priestly work of the church offered to God (Rom. 15:16). It is a task which involves much sacrifice and suffering (Col. 1:24 ff.; 2 Cor. 11:23–28; 12:10), but it is the necessary prelude to the coming of Christ in glory to reign (Mk. 13:10). It is, however, a task which is certain of success, for by the power of God a people who fear Him will be gathered out of every nation (Rom. 11:25–36; Rev. 5:9).

THE MINISTRY OF THE CHURCH

No human society ever made any headway without the appointment of certain of its members to do various tasks on behalf of the other members and to administer law and order. Thus, from a purely human point of view, it would be necessary for the church to have various ministers to carry on its work. In His wisdom God has provided that there should be such ministers in the church. Jesus Christ Himself came to be a Servant (literally, 'minister', Mk. 10:45, AV), and He is thus the pattern for the various ministers whom God appoints in His church. The ministry is, then, appointed by God (1 Cor. 12:28; Eph. 4:11) in order that His church may grow to maturity (Eph. 4:12 f.).

The priesthood of believers (Hebrews 10:19–25)

It is important to distinguish clearly between priesthood and ministry in the church. As we have already seen, the church is a priesthood and every member of it may be regarded as a priest (Rev. 1:6); thus every Christian has the right to approach God and the duty to offer himself as a sacrifice to the service of God, and he has no need of any human priest to act as his mediator before God, since Jesus Christ alone is the Mediator (Heb. 10:21). Similarly, every Christian has the right to approach God on behalf of his fellow-men in prayer (Jas. 5:16). All Christians are thus priests, and a minister in the church is no more and no less a priest than his fellow-believers.

Every Christian may also be regarded as fulfilling some task of ministry in the church for the benefit of the church as a whole (Heb. 10:24; 1 Thes. 5:11). But since the Spirit gives different gifts to different men, it is inevitable that God calls those who possess the appropriate gifts to perform special ministries within the church (1 Cor. 12:4–11). Such ministers act for the benefit of the whole church and not for personal gain (1 Pet. 5:2 f.), and they are to receive the honour appropriate to their position as servants of God (1 Thes. 5:12 f.).

A variety of ministers and ministerial tasks is mentioned in the New Testament, and no precise pattern is laid down. Clearly the Spirit guided the church according to its local needs. Since there is no clear pattern laid down, our task today is to follow out the principles laid down by the New Testament, and in practice this means that there may be as much difference of detail from church to church as there was in the New Testament churches. Nevertheless, despite these differences of detail we can distinguish three essential tasks of ministry in the church.

The ministry of the Word (2 Timothy 4:1–5)

The most important task of ministry in the church is the preaching of the Word of God. This includes the preaching of the gospel to unbelievers by evangelists and the instruction of Christians by teachers. It is customary also to include here the administration of the sacraments (cf. Acts 20:11), since for the sake of decency and order (1 Cor. 14:20) it is desirable that this task be performed by those who are authorized by the church.

The administration of discipline (Matthew 18:15–20)

A second task of ministry is the maintaining of godly discipline in the church. Since the church is composed of men and women who are still liable to sin there will always be errors of faith and life among its members, and so there must be some form of discipline to maintain the purity and holiness of the church. The ministers of the church are therefore authorized in company with the church as a whole (Mt. 18:17; 1 Cor. 5:1–5) to reprove sinners and even, if they prove impenitent, to exclude them for a time from fellowship. But such discipline is always meant to be remedial, and no effort is to be spared to restore the sinner to fellowship (2 Cor. 2:5–11). We ought perhaps to note that the New Testament writers could be very stern on this matter, especially where the truth of the gospel was at stake (2 Jn. 8–11).

The oversight of property and finance (2 Corinthians 8; 9)

From its earliest days the church felt a responsibility to look after its poorer members (Acts 2:44 f.), and it was not long before ministers were appointed to look after this matter (Acts 6:1–8). Paul himself took steps to encourage the churches he had founded to provide for the needs of the poor in Palestine (Rom. 15:27; 3 Jn. 5–8). Along with this work of charity, the church has also to provide for its full-time servants (Phil. 4:10–20; 1 Cor. 9:14) and to administer any property it may possess. Clearly ministers must be appointed for these tasks, although this does not, of course, mean men who are necessarily engaged full-time in such work.

The ordination of ministers (Acts 13:1–3)

Ordination is the rite by which the church recognizes the divine appointment of certain men to be its ministers (whether for full-time or part-time work) and accepts them as such. In the New Testament ordination was normally by the act of laying on of hands—a symbol which indicated the conferring of authority (Acts 6:6; 14:23). This act was confirmed by God who bestowed gifts of the Holy Spirit upon the minister thus appointed (1 Tim. 4:14; 2 Tim. 1:6).

The rite of ordination—in whatever form it be observed—is meant to safeguard the church from false ministers who are not called of God. It is clear that in the New Testament men were ordained only after the church had prayed and sought the guidance of the Spirit (cf. references already given).

THE MEANS OF GRACE

God's Word and gifts come to His people in various ways which are usually called 'the means of grace'. Both as individuals and in company with our fellow-Christians in the church we receive salvation by hearing the Word of God (2 Tim. 3:14–17) and by the work of the Holy Spirit in our hearts (1 Thes. 1:5 f.). There are two principal ways in which this happens—through the preaching of the gospel and through the sacraments.

The preaching of the gospel (1 Timothy 4:11–16)

It has been said that God had only one Son and He made Him a preacher. In the early church the work of Jesus in preaching was carried on as one of its principal activities. Right from the Day of Pentecost the apostles and their associates preached to unbelievers and taught believers.

The content of such preaching was not simply human words, for through it the word of God was brought to the hearers (1 Thes. 2:13). It possessed power to convert and save because the Holy Spirit was active in its proclamation (1 Thes. 1:5). Those who preached it did not rely on deceitful methods to get their message across (2 Cor. 2:17; 1 Thes. 2:5), but trusted in the power of God (2 Cor. 2:13–16) and the prayers of Christians (Eph. 6:18–20). This was the secret of their boldness and effectiveness. Such preaching produced faith in the hearers (1 Cor. 2:4 f.) and acted like spiritual milk in nourishing Christians (1 Pet. 2:2).

The sacraments (1 Corinthians 10:1–14)

The word 'sacrament' is not found in the New Testament but came into use quite early to describe the visible signs or acts which are means of grace and salvation for Christians. Two such signs are recognized by the church: baptism and the Lord's supper; they are linked together in this passage where Paul points to foreshadowings of them in the Old Testament, and both rest on the example and command of Christ Himself (Mt. 28:19; 1 Cor. 11:23–27). Ever since the Day of Pentecost they have been observed by the church (Acts 2:41 f.).

The sacraments are to be regarded as outward signs through which God makes known His love to us and we pledge ourselves to be His people (cf. the significance of circumcision in the Old Testament). They are a visible presentation of the gospel, and just as we receive the grace of God through the preaching of the word of God so we also receive grace through the sacraments of the word of God. Much confusion has been caused by thinking of 'grace' as a kind of 'stuff' given to us by God, as though along with the bread and wine of the supper God gives us a portion of 'grace'; it is more true to Scripture to think of the sacraments as ways in which God shows to us that He is gracious by acting graciously towards us. Thus the sacraments are visible signs to us that God, whom we cannot see, is gracious to us and saves us from our sins, and by receiving them we indicate openly our faith in God.

We cannot dispense with the sacraments because they are commanded by God. He has provided them for our good, so that by the most simple means He may assure us of His love for us. The sacraments are one of the ways in which God makes known His salvation to us and we signify our acceptance of His salvation. They are not the only means, nor are they the indispensable means; but ordinarily God wills that all Christians should receive these visible and sure tokens of His love.

Baptism (Acts 2:37–41)

Baptism in water was administered by John the Baptist to

all who repented and sought forgiveness of their sins in preparation for the coming of the Messiah, Jesus. He prophesied that the coming Messiah would baptize with the Holy Spirit (Mk. 1:1–8). The word 'baptism' thus refers to an immersion in or sprinkling with water, or to the reception of the Holy Spirit. There is a third way in which the word is used: Jesus spoke of His death on the cross as a baptism (Lk. 12:50). Here He was using an Old Testament metaphor in which suffering and calamity are likened to the experience of sinking into water or being swallowed up by the sea (Ps. 69:1 f., 14 f.). This probably means that because Jesus endured a baptism of suffering those who believe in Him and submit to water-baptism receive the benefits of His suffering for them.

These three points help us to understand the meaning of Christian baptism. Christian baptism is a sign that we are cleansed from our sins and forgiven (Eph. 5:26) because of what Christ has done for us, and that we receive the same Holy Spirit who descended on Christ at His baptism (Acts 2:38). A further and most important point is that baptism is 'in the name of Jesus Christ' (Acts 2:38), or 'into the body' (see 1 Cor. 12:13); this signifies that the baptized belong to Christ. They are united with Him, and in particular they become sharers in His death and resurrection (Rom. 6:1–11). Finally, they become members of the church, which is His body. Baptism by water is, in short, the outward sign of reception of the grace of God, through which a person is united by faith to Jesus Christ as his Saviour and becomes a member of God's people.

The 'conditions' for baptism are hearing the word of God, repentance for sin, and faith in Jesus Christ (Acts 2:38; 18:8). These are not 'conditions' in the sense that we must attain a certain standard in order to be fit for baptism. They are rather the characteristics of the faith which, in response to God's grace, joyfully accepts the gospel and believes in Christ.

The practice of baptizing infants (as distinct from believing children) grew up very early in the church. In view of the analogy of circumcision in the Old Testament (Col. 2:11 f.), the strong sense of family kinship in the New

Testament, by which the action of the head of the family was more or less binding on the rest of the family (Acts 16:15,34; 18:8), and the place allotted by Christ to children (Luke has 'infants') in His kingdom (Lk. 18:15–17), it was perhaps natural that infants should be baptized in Christian families as a sign that God's grace was available for them and in confidence that they would grow up to complete their baptism by conscious faith in Christ. Expositors differ, however, as to whether there is New Testament evidence for the practice of infant baptism.

The Lord's supper (1 Corinthians 10:16 f.; 11:17 ff.)

Baptism is the once-for-all symbol of our conversion and entry upon the Christian life by the grace of God; the Lord's supper is the sign of the Lord's continual grace to us, the 'bread for pilgrims'. When Jesus gathered together with His disciples for their last meal, He took the loaf of bread, gave thanks, broke it and gave it to them with the words, 'Take, eat: this is my body, which is broken for you: this do in remembrance of me.' As the meal progressed, He took the cup of red wine, gave thanks for it, and said, as He passed it round, 'This cup is the new testament in my blood: this do ye, as oft as ye drink it, in remembrance of me.' This simple rite was observed by His disciples, at first as part of a communal meal, Sunday by Sunday.

What is its meaning? Before Jesus died, when He inaugurated the feast, it was a symbol that His body was about to be broken and His blood to be shed in order that God's new covenant with the new Israel might be ratified. By giving the bread and wine to His disciples, Jesus was inviting them to share in the blessings of the new covenant. For us, now that Christ has died and risen from the dead, the Lord's supper means five things.

First, it reminds us of His death and its meaning for us. We do this in remembrance of Him, so that as we receive the bread and wine we may remember that He died for our salvation.

Second, as we give thanks to God for the bread and wine (which are in themselves symbolic of God's daily provision for our bodies), so we thank Him for the gift of salvation which they represent. That is why the supper is sometimes called the 'Eucharist' (literally, 'thanksgiving').

Third, the Bible often speaks of the life to come as a banquet (Lk. 22:29 f.). The supper is a foretaste of that banquet, for at it we show forth the Lord's death 'till he come' and until faith is replaced by sight. Thus the supper looks forward to the day of full salvation.

Fourth, Christians who look forward to communion with Christ at His heavenly table can have communion with Him here and now. He is present at His table to give us the bread and wine (cf. Mt. 18:20). The cup is a sharing in His blood and the bread is a sharing in His body (1 Cor. 10:16), so that the supper is a visible sign of the way in which we who believe in Christ are spiritually nourished by Him (Jn. 6:51–58).

Fifth, the one loaf which is shared at the supper is a symbol of the unity of God's people with each other as members of the one body (1 Cor. 10:17). At the supper where they worship and adore the one Lord Jesus Christ and receive His grace, Christians are united together in fellowship as the one people of God.

By the word of God, written in the Scriptures, preached from the pulpit and visibly symbolized in the sacraments, the people of God receive salvation through faith and live in hope of the coming of Christ in glory as their King.

QUESTIONS FOR DISCUSSION

1. 'Beyond the pale of the church no forgiveness of sins, no salvation, can be hoped for' (John Calvin): what do you think Calvin meant by this statement, and how far do you think it is justified?

2. What important facts about the nature of the church may be deduced from the description of it as the new Israel of God and the body of Christ? (See the references on pp. 71 f.).

3. 'Sir, you wish to serve God and go to heaven? Remember that you cannot serve Him alone. You must therefore find companions or make them; the Bible knows nothing of

solitary religion' (a 'serious' man to John Wesley): why is fellowship so important in the Christian life?

4. Does the New Testament teach that the task of spreading the gospel is the responsibility of every individual Christian or of the church as a whole (and thus in practice only of certain people appointed by the church)?

5. What place is there in the church today for discipline, and what form should it take?

6. What would you say was the purpose of Jesus in instituting the Lord's supper? (Consider the accounts of the Last Supper in the Gospels and 1 Corinthians 11:23–26.)

Section 7
THE LAST THINGS

Our subject in this closing section is the final intervention of God in the history of the world, bringing the present world to an end and establishing fully and finally the new order which He inaugurated at the first coming of Jesus Christ. This topic is known as 'eschatology' (literally, 'the doctrine of the last things').

THE FINAL MANIFESTATION OF GOD'S KINGLY RULE

We shall begin this section by considering the purpose of God in history and the way in which this process will finally be worked out.

The Old Testament expectation (Micah 4:1–7)

The prophets of Israel were men who were profoundly affected by the evil and injustice which they saw rampant everywhere in the world. They saw that even the people of Israel were sinners in the sight of God, and they interpreted the various disasters which overtook them as evidence of God's judgment upon His people. They were perplexed by the problem of the suffering of the innocent and the prosperity of the wicked. They longed for peace and security to be established in the earth.

In these problems and questionings they were sustained by their faith in Jehovah as the God of history, and they believed that one day He Himself would intervene in history to set up His kingly rule among men and to establish truth and justice among men. They looked forward to a day when Jerusalem would be the centre of a peaceful world, in which the offspring of David would rule the nations and bring salvation to all men. In short, they believed that God Himself would personally intervene in the last days to establish His rule among men (Is. 9:1–7; 11:1–9).

The dawn of the new era (Luke 1:68–79)

In the fullness of time God sent His Son, Jesus the Messiah, to inaugurate His kingly rule amongst men. Jesus proclaimed that the kingdom of God was at hand, and evidence was not lacking that God had intervened in the life of the world: the coming of Jesus was attended by signs and wonders which caused people to say 'God has visited his people' (Lk. 7:16), and after His death and resurrection the Holy Spirit was poured out upon the church (cf. Joel 2:28–32). Jesus summoned men to enter the kingdom, and after His death His disciples proclaimed the same gospel of salvation through faith in Him.

The new era had in fact arrived; for all who had eyes to see, God had come among His people in power. Nevertheless, not all believed the good news, and outwardly the world did not appear to be very different. Thus our present age is a kind of period of transition; the old era has been judged and is doomed to end, and the new era has already come upon us, so that Christians who live in the old era are already members of the new era. In His mercy, God has provided this 'interval' before He makes a final end of the old era, so that all men may hear the gospel and have the opportunity of becoming citizens of the new era.

The important point is that the end has already begun. The promises of God have begun to be fulfilled in Jesus Christ, and the power of the new era is already at work. Consequently, the first coming of Jesus is proof that God will one day bring the old era to a full end and Himself reign over the men of the new era. Christians, therefore, look forward to the completion of God's mighty act begun at the first coming of Jesus Christ.

The full arrival of the new era (2 Peter 3:1–14)

God has begun His reign! That is the meaning of the first coming of Jesus. But we do not yet see all things subjected to Him; the world is not yet the place which the Old Testament prophets envisaged. God is not yet the open and acknowledged King, but evil and injustice still hold sway. But the New Testament promises that God, who has begun to rule in Jesus Christ, will one day rule over all men; the present evil age will come to an end, and God will establish a new heaven and a new earth in which righteousness dwells. In that day God will judge all men according to their works and those who submit to His rule will become citizens of the New Jerusalem, the city of God, and reign with Him for ever. All this He will accomplish at the second coming of His Son, Jesus Christ, the Saviour and the Judge of all men.

We must now look more closely at this great event.

THE SECOND COMING OF THE LORD JESUS CHRIST

The advent of Jesus Christ (Titus 2:11–14)

The fact of the second coming of Christ is abundantly attested in the New Testament; the details of that coming are very obscure, and nobody will wish to dogmatize about them. The reason for this is that so stupendous an event as the winding up of human history can only be described in symbolic language, just as we can only describe the nature of God Himself by means of symbols. While we can have some indication from these symbols as to the nature of the second coming, it is most unwise to interpret them all literally or to read our own ideas into them. Failure to observe this fact has given rise to much unwarranted speculation. Here, therefore, we shall do little more than stress the fact of the second coming of Jesus.

Jesus Himself spoke clearly of His second coming as Ruler and Judge of all men (Mt. 25:31 ff.; Mk. 8:38; 13:26; 14:62; Lk. 17:22–37). He indicated that it would be preceded by various events—the rise of false Saviours, the persecution of His people and the increase of human wickedness (Mk. 13:1–25; cf. 2 Thes. 2:3–12; 2 Tim. 3:12 f.), but He stated that nobody could calculate the date of His coming (Lk. 17:20 f.; Acts 1:7), and that only the Father knew when it would be (Mk. 13:32).

The apostles also believed in the second coming of Christ and instructed their converts to live a holy life in preparation for that day (Acts 3:19–21; Phil. 3:20 f.; 4:5; Col. 3:4 f.;

1 Thes. 1:9 f.; 2 Tim. 4:1 f.; Heb. 9:28; 1 Pet. 1:7; 1 Jn. 2:28; Rev. 1:7). Their concern was not that men should sit and wait for the day, but that they should live in a manner befitting servants awaiting the arrival of their master (cf. Lk. 12:35–48).

The final manifestation of evil (2 Thessalonians 2:3–12)

The New Testament indicates that the second coming of Christ will be preceded by the final effort of evil to overcome God. Before the end of world history Satan will make his last attempt to overthrow Christ. Paul speaks of a figure called antichrist, while John emphasizes that there are many antichrists already at work in the world (1 Jn. 2:18). In the last book of the Bible there is a description of a battle between God and Satan (Rev. 19:11–21; 20:7–10). The precise meaning of these prophecies is not known to us.

The problem of the millennium (Revelation 20:1–6)

There is one passage in the New Testament which refers to a reign of Christ and His saints for a thousand years (i.e. a millennium). The meaning of this passage is as obscure as anything in the New Testament, as is shown by the multitude of interpretations offered by scholars. Three main views are held, known, as pre-, post- and a-millennialism. The **first** is that the second coming of Christ precedes His reign with His saints (including dead Christians who have been resurrected) for a thousand years, after which will follow the general resurrection of the rest of the dead, the day of judgment, and the life of heaven. The **second** is that the second coming of Christ is ushered in by the ultimate triumph of the gospel in the world, and this triumphal period is the millennium. The **third** is that the description in Revelation 20 is entirely symbolical and that *no* literal thousand-year reign is to be expected other than the present era beginning with Christ's ascension and exaltation. There is as yet no agreement among Christians as to which of these views does fullest justice to the New Testament teaching.

Jesus as Judge and Saviour (1 John 2:28–3:3)

The second coming of Jesus is His coming as Judge of all

men. The New Testament speaks sometimes of God and sometimes of Christ as Judge (Rom. 14:10 ff.; Phil. 2:10 f.), since God has committed all judgment to Christ (Jn. 5:22; Acts 17:30 f.). In that day Christ will judge every man according to his works and words (Rom. 2:5–11; 2 Cor. 5:10; Mt. 12:36 f.); this, of course, is not a denial of the principle of justification by faith, for we have already seen that the evidence of faith is good works and that only those who have put their faith in Christ can perform works acceptable to God. The judgment will also be upon Christians; there will be reward or loss for the way in which they have used their talents (Mt. 25:14–30; 1 Cor. 3:12–15).

The second coming of Christ also means that He appears as the Saviour of His people. On that day they will be transformed to be like Him; they will no longer be harassed by temptation and they will be made perfectly holy (Phil. 3:21; 1 Thes. 3:13; 1 Jn. 3:2). They will take their seats at His table and reign with Him for ever (Mt. 8:11; Lk. 22:30; Rev. 22:5).

THE RESURRECTION OF THE DEAD

Closely associated with the second coming of Christ is the resurrection of the dead.

The intermediate state (Philippians 1:21–26)

The problem of the condition of the dead before resurrection is shrouded in obscurity. If the parable of the rich man and Lazarus (Lk. 16:19 ff.) is to be taken as referring to this (which is not certain), we may be entitled to deduce from it that a separation already exists between believers and unbelievers, the former being at peace and the latter in torment. But it may be wrong to interpret the parable literally.

As regards believers, Paul evidently regards them as with Christ (Phil. 1:23) and speaks of those who sleep 'by Jesus' (see 1 Thes. 4:14). The penitent thief went to paradise with Jesus (Lk. 23:43), and Stephen saw Jesus standing in heaven to receive him (Acts 7:55–59). All this suggests that death ushers a Christian into the presence of Christ. Beyond that we cannot go, and as regards the unrighteous the New Testament is virtually silent.

Resurrection and transformation (1 Corinthians 15:35–57)

At the second coming of Christ two important events take place. First, the dead who are in Christ are raised up and join the triumphal train of Christ (1 Thes. 4:14–17). Second, Christians who are alive at His coming are caught up to meet Him in the air.

All who participate in this event are transformed by the power of God and receive a new body. Since flesh and blood cannot inherit the eternal kingdom of God and immortality, Christians receive a new 'spiritual' body (1 Cor. 15:44); just as a seed 'dies' and gives place to a plant which is organically related to it but very different in appearance, so our present fleshly bodies will give place to new and perfect spiritual bodies fit for the life of heaven.

What this means is beyond our comprehension, although we may perhaps draw an analogy from the transfigured and resurrected body of Christ (Mk. 9:2 f.; Lk. 24:39). The life of heaven is to be a continuation on a more grand and glorious scale of life in Christ on earth.

The fate of unbelievers (2 Thessalonians 1:5–10)

Those who are not members of Christ's people do not share in the transformation which characterizes the resurrection of Christians. Nevertheless, they do appear before God and Christ on the day of judgment (Mt. 25:41 ff.; Jn. 5:28 f.; Acts 24:15; Rev. 20:11–15). The judgment which has already been passed on them in this life is ratified (Jn. 3:18 f.), and they suffer the punishment of exclusion from the presence of God. Opinions differ as to whether this means eternal torment or annihilation. Those who adopt the latter alternative stress that it does not minimize the severity of God's judgment on the wicked, annihilation being a fate sufficiently dreadful in itself.

A word should possibly be added here about those who have never heard the gospel of salvation. The New Testament does not speculate much on this matter; rather, it commands the church of God to preach the gospel to all men so that they may enjoy salvation both here and hereafter. Yet it is hinted that the heathen will be judged according to the light which they have. There are some grounds for holding that men whose way of life is such that they would have accepted Christ if they had heard of Him will surely be saved at the last day because the sacrifice of Christ avails for them also (Rom. 2:12–16; cf. also Mt. 25:31 ff.). What we may be quite sure of is the great mercy and utter justice of God who desires all men to be saved and come to a knowledge of the truth (1 Tim. 2:4).

THE LIFE OF HEAVEN

As with all the matters which we have discussed in this chapter the life hereafter can be described only in symbol, but we can make two significant assertions about it.

The new heaven and the new earth (Revelation 21:1–21)

With the day of judgment comes the end of the present world system which is corrupted by sin and evil (Rom. 8:19–23). The old era ends and the new era replaces it. A new earth and heaven are provided, in which dwells righteousness (2 Pet. 3:13). The new home of redeemed men and women is spoken of as a new Jerusalem, for it is the holy city to which the earthly, sinful Jerusalem points. Gone for ever are sin and sorrow, and eternal bliss is the lot of God's people. The old has passed away, all is made new.

Life in the presence of God (Revelation 21:22 – 22:5)

The life of heaven is what it is precisely because it is life in the presence of God. The fellowship between man and his Creator which was broken by sin is fully restored. The presence of God among His people is no longer confined to His temple, as in the Old Testament, or to His unseen presence among believers, as in the New Testament, but He is in the midst of His people and they see His face. Both the Father and His Son, the Lamb, are the light of the heavenly Jerusalem, and the Spirit of God summons men to enter the city (Rev. 22:17). Thus finally redeemed men and women enter into that fellowship of love which binds Father, Son and Spirit together, and the holy love of God becomes the final and victorious reality (1 Cor. 13:13). God is at last all in all (1 Cor. 15:28).

QUESTIONS FOR DISCUSSION

1. What effect should the hope of the second coming of Jesus have upon our Christian lives? (See the references on pp. 85 f.).

2. 'My desire is to depart and be with Christ, for that is far better' (Phil. 1:23): what should be the attitude of the Christian to this world and its joys in the light of such a statement as this?

3. Would you say that the prophecy of a new heaven and earth to replace this present universe makes the facts of human progress and history to be ultimately of no real importance? Is the Christian merely a stranger and pilgrim in this world with no real interest in its activities and affairs?

4. How would you reconcile the New Testament teaching that justification is by faith and the final judgment is by works?

5. What indications does the New Testament give of the transformation which takes place for Christians at the resurrection of the dead? (See 1 Corinthians 15:35 ff. and 2 Corinthians 5:1–10.)

6. 'In a universe of love there can be no heaven which tolerates a chamber of horrors, no hell for any which does not at the same time make it a hell for God' (J. A. T. Robinson): do you think that this is a fair criticism of the New Testament doctrine of the final destiny of the wicked?

BOOKS FOR FURTHER READING

(All are IVP books unless otherwise indicated.)

GENERAL

T. C. Hammond, **In Understanding Be Men.**

Evangelical Belief. An explanation of the doctrinal basis of the IVF.

SECTION 1

J. Stafford Wright, **The Authority of the Bible.**

R. M. Horn, **The Book that Speaks for Itself.**

SECTION 2

R. T. France, **The Living God.**

K. Runia, **I Believe in God . . .** (Tyndale Press).

SECTION 3

J. N. Hawthorne, **Questions of Science and Faith.**

H. Silvester, **Arguing with God.**

SECTION 4

J. R. W. Stott, **Basic Christianity.**

L. Morris, **The Lord From Heaven.**

F. Colquhoun, **The Meaning of the Cross.**

J. N. D. Anderson, **The Evidence for the Resurrection.**

M. Green, **Man Alive!**

I. H. Marshall, **The Work of Christ** (Paternoster Press).

SECTION 5

J. Philip, **Repentance.**

Christian Maturity.

L. Morris, **Spirit of the Living God.**

G. Campbell Morgan, **The Life of the Christian** (Pickering and Inglis).

J. R. W. Stott, **Men Made New,** an exposition of Romans 5–8.

K. F. W. Prior, **The Way of Holiness.**
J. Oswald Sanders, **The Holy Spirit of Promise** (Marshall, Morgan and Scott).

SECTION 6

A. M. Stibbs, **God's Church.**
D. M. Lloyd-Jones, **The Basis of Christian Unity.**
L. Morris, **Ministers of God.**

SECTION 7

G. T. Manley, **The Return of Jesus Christ.**

INDEX OF SCRIPTURE PASSAGES FOR STUDY